Fifth Edition

Welcome to an educational and entertaining encounter with your RV's "unique" appliances. This *Primer* was explicitly designed to get all RVers thinking in a *different* direction.

Written for all RV enthusiasts, especially those who are:
- Initially "CONSIDERING" RVing,
- Just "BEGINNING" their RVing experience,
- Have been "CAMPING for YEARS," or,
- Living the dream of "FULL-TIMING."

The information within will clearly demonstrate that living with electricity in an RV is NOT the same as living with electricity in a house. Further, it will explain why electrical "things" don't seem to function in an RV the way you might expect them to (i.e., as they do in your home).

This *Primer* endeavors to help all readers establish a practical awareness of "basic" 120-Volt RV Electricity. Principally, a knowledge level that will enable each reader to start thinking in terms of "electrical cause and effect"— thus preventing the proverbially frustrating, "OH, NO! NOW, WHAT?" when everything in the RV suddenly "quits," and you have no idea why?

The included Editorial *Comments* are based on the author's sixty years of experience using and living in RVs (including more than a decade of recent "full-time" RVing) and conducting the business of repairing RVs. Now, he is concentrating on educating the RV owners.

The ladies are especially encouraged to read everything between this book's covers. Then, they will understand where their partner's logic went wrong and confidently be able to "suggest" a different approach.

SP20183g

Understanding Your RV's "SHORE POWER"

120-Volt Electricity

- - A Primer - -

by

Dale Lee Sumner

Retired Master Certified RV Service Technician

Fifth Edition

Copyright © 2020 by Dale Lee Sumner

All rights reserved. No part of this book may be reproduced or transmitted in any form by any means, electronic or mechanical, including photocopying and recording, or by any information storage and retrieval system, without permission in writing from the publisher, except in the case of brief quotations embodied in critical reviews or articles.

Published by SUMDALUS-USA
sales.sumdalus-usa@outlook.com

Printed in the United States of America
ISBN: 978-0-9974634-8-4

Cover Image – by Author

<u>Other Published RV **"Primer"** books
available from **www.sumdalus.com**</u>

Understanding Your RV's "APPLIANCES"
Refrigerator, Furnace, Water Heater, and Rooftop Air Conditioner

Understanding Your RV's "BATTERY POWER"
12 Volt Electricity

Understanding Your RV's "HOLDING TANKS"
Bio-Waste Management

My RV "LOGBOOK"
A Vital Record of My RV's Equipment & Appliance Information

Dedicated to

My father.

He enthusiastically enjoyed working for a total of 41 years as an Aviation Electronics (Avionics) Technician. (20 in the Navy and 21 with the Federal Aviation Agency)

A man of quiet, subtle humor, he conspicuously displayed the government's retirement plaque which lauded his

"40 Years and 12 Months
Combined Civil Service
to the American People"

(He refused to give it back to be corrected.)

A true Jack-of-all-Trades, and rightfully a Master-at-Most, he was well-known as a walking encyclopedia when it came to things mechanical or electrical. He was always willing to "try anything new, at least once." And usually did.

My father began explaining the basics of electricity to me when I was about six years old. He also introduced me to the workings of our first RV when I was thirteen. Because of his infectious enthusiasm and example, I, too, take pleasure in figuring out "what makes things tick," as well as "looking for interesting correlations," which result in better comprehension of a subject.

Rest in Peace, Dad. I'm still learning something new, every day!

ACKNOWLEDGMENT

I am especially thankful to Mr. Robert Schneider, a one-time co-owner and lead engineer of Progressive Industries. His depth of knowledge about RV electricity and the need for electrical protection is unsurpassed. His willingness to introduce me to a more in-depth knowledge level of RV electricity has certainly been a great asset to my education and professional proficiency. Thank you so much, Robert!!

DISCLAIMER

The text, photos, diagrams, and analogies within this book are meant to guide the reader toward a better understanding of the 120 VAC electrical system associated with a Recreational Vehicle (RV). They may not be complete, may contain minor errors, and may not apply accurately to an owner's specific problem. They are not to be relied upon as guidance for repairing anyone's RV's electrical systems or components. All RV owners are responsible for any hazards they encounter or produce if they work on their RV's electrical system. The legal right to work on some parts of your system may be limited in your state. Contacting a local RV Dealership to schedule a "bring it in" appointment or contacting a local, Independent RV Service Technician to "come to" an RV site are always options. Either one may be required to accomplish necessary repairs.

NOTE

Most photographs, images, diagrams, or charts not sourced/credited within this *Primer* were designed and/or produced by the author. The publisher has made every reasonable effort to contact all copyright holders. Any errors which may have occurred are inadvertent. Anyone who, for any reason, has not been contacted is invited to communicate with the publisher so that a full acknowledgment may be made in subsequent editions of this work.

INTRODUCTION

Open any textbook about electricity, and you will find some rather daunting, traditional abbreviations and definitions similar to the following:

A – Amperage (Amps). A unit of electrical current (Also Known As [a.k.a.] Amp Draw or Current Flow.)

AC – Alternating Current. An electric current that reverses its charge in a circuit at regular intervals/cycles. (Electrical power produced by the power company, your generator, or your inverter is called alternating current.) Graphically represented as: ∿ (Not to be confused with Air Conditioning which is traditionally abbreviated as A/C.)

DC – Direct Current. An electric current that flows only in one (1) direction. (Electrical power supplied by your converter/charger or drawn from your battery system is referred to as direct current.) Graphically represented as: ≡≡≡ or ▬

V – Voltage (Volts). A unit of electrical potential/pressure.

W – Wattage (Watts). A unit of electrical power.

120 VAC – Standard notation for 120-<u>V</u>olts of <u>A</u>lternating <u>C</u>urrent.

12 VDC – Standard notation for 12-<u>V</u>olts of <u>D</u>irect <u>C</u>urrent.

A *Primer* (pronounced **prĭm'**-ər [rhymes with "trimmer"]) is defined by Webster's II New Riverside Dictionary as "a small book covering the fundamentals of a topic." (FYI: Webster's also defines a **'prī-mər** (rhymes with "chimer") as a substance used to prime a surface or ignite an explosive charge.)

This "small book" concentrates on the 120-Volt electrical system in your RV. It is not intended to be a high-level, scientifically correct, know-all, or end-all document to satisfy the most critical of electrical engineers. In their own right, they are operating at a different level of expertise than the rest of us. Instead, it is written to provide the typical RVer (*J.* [Jane or John] *Q. Public*) with a baseline understanding of the electrical system that operates the most prominent equipments/appliances inside their RV.

Within these pages, I have used ordinary, everyday examples to demonstrate concepts that will hopefully provide you with a fundamental understanding of RV electricity. The analogies may not be 100% correct, but I believe they get the point across.

Foremost, within these pages, I sincerely try to influence each reader to take a different view from how you "automatically" use electricity as it applies to buildings to how you must approach electricity "logically" when it pertains to RVs. House/Commercial electricity usage is one thing, but using electricity in an RV is something else. Guaranteed!

Your home was probably built some time ago. It is static – does not move. The electrical wiring was installed to a specific set of codes (city/county/state). Unless you have remodeled or built on an addition, the wiring has been undisturbed. While the electric company's name might have changed from time to time, the actual physical (<u>permanent</u>) electrical connection to the grid has probably always been the same since day one. Using electricity within your home is so commonplace, you don't even think about it when you turn "ON" a switch. You simply "hit" the switch and always expect everything to work. Now, that's blind faith.

Living in an RV is vastly different. The RV is exceptionally mobile. And who knows what the bumps and jolts of the highway have done to some of your internal electrical connections? Yes, the wiring was installed per a specific code, but the wiring set-up and code (national only) are different from those for a house. Whenever you go somewhere in your RV, you establish a new (temporary) connection to the electrical grid, most times supplied by a different power company. When you "flip" a switch "ON," are you activating the 120-Volt system or the 12-Volt system? Are you wired for 30 or 50 Amp Service? Did you have to adapt "up" or "down" in order to "plug in" to available power? Do you know what causes the Voltage to "drop?" Or, what causes the Amp Draw to shoot up high enough to "trip" the Circuit Breaker at the Post? (BTW: Our boating friends prefer to call it a Pedestal instead of a Post.)

There is obviously much more to pay attention to in an RV than in a building when it comes to electricity. And this was the driving reason for writing this *Primer*. I hope the analogies capture your attention, but, most importantly, I sincerely hope, when you have finished reading this book, you can honestly say, "Wow, I learned something!" or even, "Now... it makes sense!"

BEFORE YOU CONTINUE...

On the next page, I have a little quiz for you to take. And it is essential that you **do** take the quiz. It's intended to help you establish a "baseline" of your current knowledge of electricity as it pertains to RVs. After you've graded your quiz, you'll understand why I asked you to take it.

It's just ten (10) simple, True or False questions. If you don't know the answer right away, make your best, educated guess. You might surprise yourself.

So, please, find a pencil and turn the page. Thank you.

Whaddaya know 'bout...your RV's 120-Volt Electrical System?

Circle True or False

1.   T F In an RV, the 120 VAC electrical system is more important than the 12 VDC electrical system.

2.   T F RV electrical wiring codes are the same as House electrical wiring codes.

3.   T F Reverse Polarity is nothing to really worry about – everything still works.

4.   T F A 'SURGE' is the most hazardous electrical condition from which you need to protect your RV.

5.   T F An Autoformer (a.k.a. Voltage Booster/Regulator) is the best electrical protection you can get.

6.   T F There is only a 20 Amp difference between a 30 Amp RV and a 50 Amp RV.

7.   T F You can operate (turn "ON") everything electrical in your RV when your generator is on-line (running).

8.   T F All inverters must be turned "OFF" when you are plugged into shore power.

9.   T F Only exterior electrical receptacles need GFCI protection.

10.   T F The Ground Wire may be bonded or connected to the Neutral Wire at the Circuit Breaker Panel.

Now, that wasn't so hard, was it? Curious about the correct answers? I'm sure you are; however, you'll have to keep reading to determine if your answers are accurate. (I've hidden the Answer Key somewhere within the body of this book. You'll find it!)

All right, then, now that you've finished your "baseline" quiz, let's get started finding out more about your RV's "Shore Power" (120-Volt Electricity)

and why it is potentially "dangerous" to your onboard equipment, appliances, and you. . .

First, let's talk about **WATER**!! Yes, that's right, water. How water works is a concept which everyone understands. You can see, touch, hear, taste, and even play in it. Water is not a mystery.

Everyone knows about the city water supply connection at the campsite. It is a water valve (often referred to as a "water bibb") we attach a hose to in order to get water into the RV. When we rotate a valve handle all the way counter-clockwise, twist a 'T' handle, or lift a lever handle, water spews out of the valve. The water comes out because, somewhere up the line, there is a pump running to build up the pressure in the supply piping. When any valve in the system is opened, the water is pushed out. We can measure this pressure with a pressure gauge (a measuring device with an incremented dial indicator). The gauge shows us the amount of water pressure available in pounds per square inch (PSI).

We can also measure the amount of water flowing out of the valve in gallons per minute (GPM). A stopwatch and a 5-gallon bucket/pail would facilitate testing this measure-ment. (**Comment:** Although the RV's water pump uses 12 VDC to run, it is "rated" in terms of GPM.)

We know about the water pressure and flow rate, so let's say we want to build a functioning model of a grist mill and use water as a power source. Using a flume, paddle wheel, and some gearing, we know we can regulate the number of revolutions per minute (RPM). The millstone rotates by controlling either the water pressure or flow rate. With experi-mentation, we would quickly realize the stone must turn at different RPM rates to grind corn samples efficiently and thoroughly into coarse meal (slow RPMs) or wheat into fine flour (rapid RPMs).

Conceptually, we can describe our "working" grist mill model with the following "easy" mathematical expression of a Law of Physics:

POWER = PRESSURE x FLOW
(RPM)　　　　(PSI)　　　　(GPM)

We can even extend the availability of water power to another location by attaching a long hose to the water valve. And, we can also get water power from one source to two different locations by using a "**wye**" splitter and a second length of hose. If the far ends of the hoses attached to the "wye" were capped off with pressure gauges, we would see the same amount of water pressure is available at the ends of both hoses.

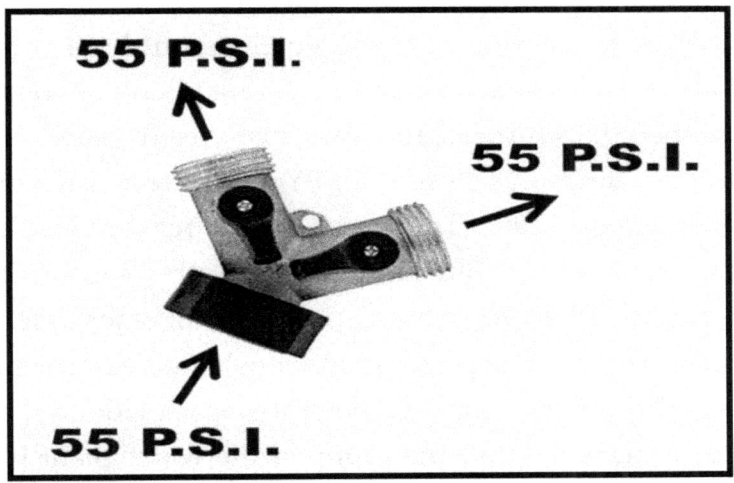

Both Outlet sides are pressurized equally!

If we add water nozzles to the ends of both hoses, we can easily control the flow, "ON" and "OFF."

(**Sidebar:** My wife and I use this wye connection concept whenever we stop at a campground or State/National Park. First, we attach a water Wye to the city water supply valve. A short hose runs from one of the wye's outlets to the city water connection on the RV for interior water. And from the other outlet, a longer hose with an attached water nozzle is carefully coiled and "charged" [i.e., the water valve is open, but the nozzle is closed] next to the water bibb. The longer hose is our "ready-to-go" <u>emergency firehose</u>! [**Comment:** With a 50-foot hose (or two connected 25-foot hoses), you could reach any location on your RV with "emergency" water, or you could use this long hose to wash the RV.])

(**Caution:** I do not recommend using a wye to run one hose to the city water connection and another to the black tank flush connection. Definitely, **NOT** a sanitary thing to do!)

Nevertheless, to continue with the water lesson about two hoses with water nozzles attached, an interesting phenomenon occurs – if you open both nozzles, the flow increases (more GPM), but the pressure decreases (less PSI). You can test this yourself. Open one nozzle fully. The water stream reaches out quite a distance from you. But, if you open the second nozzle simultaneously, the two water streams will not reach as far away as just one stream. The pressure obviously decreased when we increased the flow rate (opened both nozzles), evidenced by less distance). That's because the pump at the water plant is set to only build up a finite amount of pressure. Therefore, the water stream cannot be pushed out as far when two nozzles are open on the same water source.

The concept of one measurement going "up" (↑) while the other goes "down" (↓) is another simple Law of Physics. And that, my friends, is something we cannot change; we just have to live with it.

Now, let's take what we understand about water and apply this knowledge to electricity.

Because there is a conceptual parallel between the two systems, the following few pages contain some basic "function" correlations between them, which will help you make the transition from one system to the other.

An Electrical Outlet has the same function as a Water Valve.

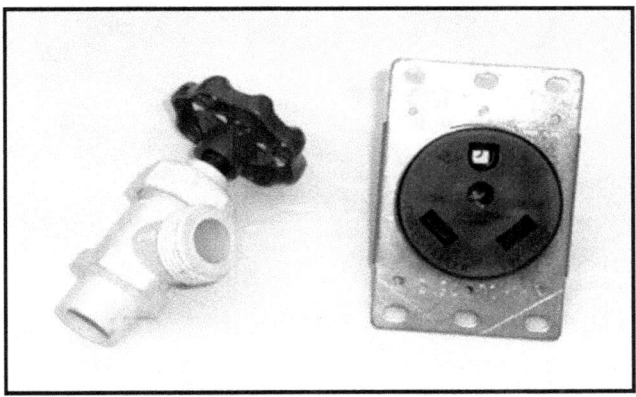

Each provides a connection point to the relevant resource.

A Voltmeter has the same function as a Pressure Gauge.

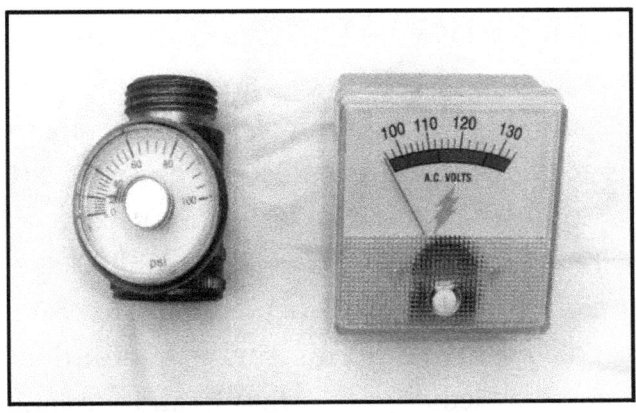

Each indicates the resource's "pressure."

A Circuit Breaker has a similar function as a Pressure Regulator.

Each is a safety device: a Circuit Breaker protects the wiring and appliances from High Current Flow, while a Pressure Regulator protects the water hose and internal plumbing from High Water Pressure.

WARNING: The water system in your RV is intended to only operate at a maximum of 50 psi (older RVs with 3/8" plumbing) or 60 psi (newer RVs with 1/2" plumbing). Water pressure can be very exasperating: sometimes dangerously high and other times aggravatingly low. Additionally, it can be strangely different between campsites in the same campground. (**Comment:** I've come across quite a few city water pressures as high as 120 psi. As a safety measure, before connecting a hose to any water valve [bibb], I strongly recommend you **ALWAYS** install a pressure regulator **FIRST**. This simple precaution will help prevent many particularly frustrating and damaging water leaks. GUARANTEED!)

An Electrical Wire has the same function as a Water Hose.

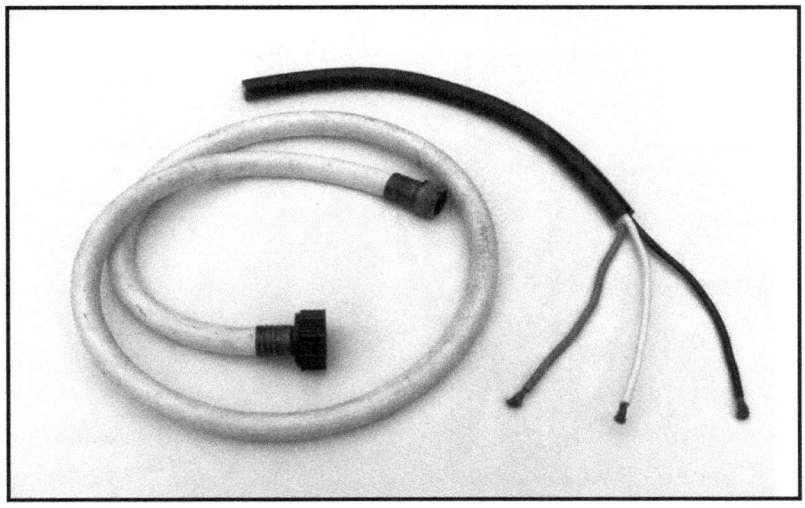

Each allows us to route the resource to a location remote from the local source (Valve/Outlet).

An Electrical Switch has the same function as a Water Nozzle.

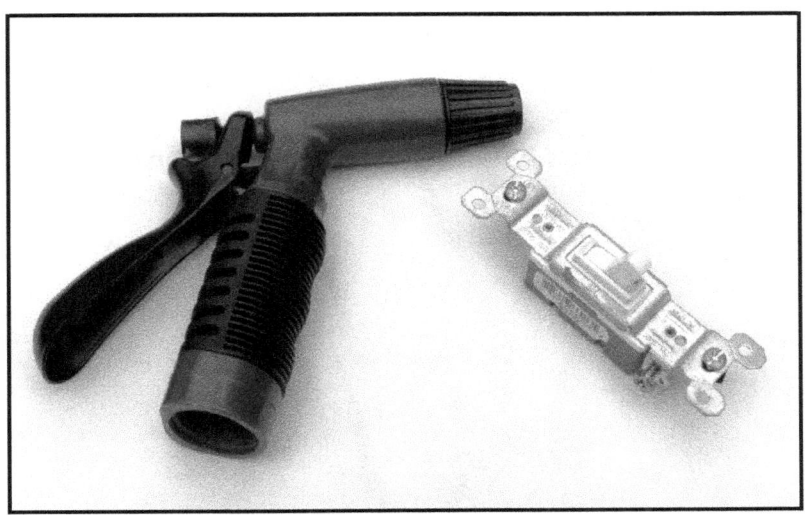

Each allows us to turn the resource "ON" and "OFF."

An Adapter has the same function
as a Water Wye (Splitter).

Each has the ability to distribute the resource's "pressure"
from one path, <u>equally</u> through two attached paths.
(The 'hot' side of a 30M to 50F Adapter's
internal workings is on the right.)

WOW! How cool was that transition?
Pretty simple. Right?

Answer Key: All the test questions on page viii are <u>False</u>! Please read page 135 at the end of this book.

Now, here is your first lesson about 120-Volt "SHORE POWER."

FUNDAMENTAL FACT: *In an RV, we do <u>NOT</u> consume electricity like we consume propulsion fuel or LP gas. We simply "borrow" it. It comes into the RV, runs our equipment, and then returns to the grid.*

A "grid" refers to the network of electric wires between the power generating plant and the electricity users – some of the grid is underground – especially in campgrounds.

In addition to the definitions listed in the Introduction to this book, here are three **more terminologies** that are necessary to know and understand:

1. An **Outlet** is a "female" receptacle we plug into to obtain the electricity that will energize our electrical appli-ance(s). The Outlet is connected to the power supply. (**Comment:** Outlets are often, although incorrectly, referred to as plugs.)

2. A **Plug** (a.k.a. Plug Head) is a "male" fitting, with metal prongs/tines, which is attached to the loose end of a Power Cord. (The other end is attached to the electrical appliance – in our most significant case, to the RV.)

3. To make a **Connection**, we push the <u>Plug Head</u> into the <u>Outlet</u> to establish a secure link/tie/bond to the power supply. Only the Plug Head is your part of the connection. Unless the Outlet is located at <u>your</u> home, it belongs to someone else (e.g., the campground) – so, remember, keep your fingers and tools <u>out</u> of it! (See Appendix # 1 for important information.)

Contrary to popular belief, electricity is <u>not</u> magic. However, for the most part, it <u>is</u> invisible. You can't see it unless it's where it doesn't belong – outside of the wiring – then it arcs and sparks. You cannot touch it unless you put your fingers or tools somewhere they do not belong – more arcs and sparks. You can't hear it unless it is arcing and sparking. You can only taste it if you have gotten an electrical "shock." And you certainly don't want to play with it unless you have a death wish.

Sorry. The previous paragraph wasn't meant to scare you away from electricity; it was intended to make sure you develop and maintain a healthy respect for electricity. Accidents can happen when dealing with electricity, but, please, don't deliberately try to antagonize it – it bites back pretty hard!

Electricity is, basically, broken down into three working parts:

1. Electrical <u>Pressure</u> is what we receive from the power company (commonly referred to as "electricity"). It is measured in **VOLT**s. The optimal pressure (Voltage) from the power company is 120 VAC. (**Remember:** The water pump.)

2. Electrical <u>Flow</u> (current) is the movement of "electricity" through wires and appliances. It is measured in **AMP**s (amperes). Flow is also referred to as "draw" – i.e., Amp Draw = Current Flow. Something <u>must</u> be turned "ON" to cause flow. (**Remember:** The water nozzle)

3. Electrical <u>Power</u> is measured in **WATT**s. All equipment is rated at a specific Wattage – this is a <u>constant value</u>. Wattage represents the real power performing the work (makes the appliance function), not the Voltage or Amperage. (**Remember:** The consistent rpm rate in order to grind wheat efficiently and thoroughly into fine flour.)

While the Law of Physics states:

$$\text{WATTS} = \text{VOLTS} \times \text{AMPS}$$

(Power = Pressure × Flow)

(Hmm...where did we see this before?)

A Law of Mathematics states:

The value(s) on the Left Side of the Equal (=) Sign **must** balance with the amount(s) on the Right Side. **SO**..., since Wattage (a constant) is on the left of the = Sign and Volts and Amps (both variables) are multiplied together on the right of the = Sign; if Amp Draw goes ↑, then, in order to mathematically balance, the Voltage must go ↓! (Turning "ON" equipment causes the Voltage to go "<u>*down*</u>." And... If Amp Draw goes ↓, then Voltage must go ↑! (Turning "OFF" equipment causes the Voltage to go "<u>*up*</u>.")

Obviously, Volts and Amps have an inverse (opposite) effect on each other!! And they must, in order to accurately exist within the applicable Laws of Physics and Mathematics.

To demonstrate this principle, let's arithmetically change the equation. Yes, that's right. Just like in 9th-grade math class – we divide both sides of the equation by Volts – and the Volts on the right of the equal (=) Sign cancel out. Now we can figure the Amp Draw for a 1500 Watt appliance (e.g., a coffee maker, water heater element, or portable electric heater) at different Voltages:

$$\frac{1500 \text{ Watts}}{120 \text{ Volts}} = 12.5 \text{ Amps}$$

$$\frac{1500 \text{ Watts}}{110 \text{ Volts}} = 13.6 \text{ Amps}$$

$$\frac{1500 \text{ Watts}}{100 \text{ Volts}} = 15.0 \text{ Amps}$$

As you can see in the equations on the previous page, the same piece of equipment (Constant Wattage) draws different Amps at different Voltages. The lower the Voltage, the higher the Amp Draw! And, vice versa – the lower the Amp Draw, the higher the Voltage.

Let's extend this theory to a larger scale. Would it make sense to say that multiple appliances, all operating at Low Voltage on the same electrical system, will result in a remarkably High Amp Draw? <u>Yes</u>, it would, and, be assured, the resultant High Amp Draw will occur very quickly.

AND an interesting phenomenon occurs here, too. If we consider Normal Amp Draw to be identified as the number of Amps drawn by a piece of equipment at the standard 120-Volt level, higher than Normal Amp Draw will result in higher heat generation as the increased Current Flow of electricity passes through the wiring and appliances. And, not surprisingly, this heat kills electronic components! (More on this later.)

Typical Amp Draws at 120-Volts (depending on equipment manufacturer):

> One (1) Heat Pump/Air Conditioner – 10 to 16 Amps.
> Electric Water Heater Element – 11.6 to 12.5 Amps.
> Microwave – 13 to 16 Amps.
> Convection Oven – 15 to 20 Amps.
> Coffee Maker – 10 to 12.5 Amps.
> Toaster – 7 to 10 Amps,
> Hair Dryer – 12.5 to 16.2 Amps.
> Space Heater – 12.5 to 15 Amps.

Observably, <u>another correlation</u>: Any equipment which generates heat, as a function of the power usage, <u>causes</u> High Current Flow!!

Are you checking your "at this moment" available Voltage level before turning "ON" additional equipment? Do you need to????

<u>YES</u>!!!! And, here's WHY:

The **National Electrical Manufacturer's Association (NEMA)** has established the **<u>Voltage Design</u> <u>Spec</u>** for electronic/electrical equipment, used in the USA, to be:

Maximum Voltage - - <u>**132 Volts**</u>
Minimum Voltage - - <u>**104 Volts**</u>

Here's how they arrived at those numbers:

Remembering our nominal Voltage Standard is 120-Volts:
120-Volts ± 10% → 120 + 12 = **132** and 120 − 12 = <u>108</u>.

The "old" standard was 110 Volts: 110 Volts ± 10% → 110 + 11 = 121 and 110 − 11 = <u>99</u>.

104 splits the difference at the bottom ends (it's halfway between 108 & 99).

(104 is also the lower end for a short-lived "middle" standard of 115 Volts)

And, now, you ask, "Why is having a standard for upper and lower Voltage levels so important?"

Let's look at **<u>Maximum Voltage</u>** first. To do so, we're going to equate it to something we all have heard about – blood pressure. Let's just look at the Systolic measurement (the upper number); it is the magnitude of the pressure in the arteries when the heart beats (when the heart muscle contracts). Normal blood pressure is judged to be between 90 and 120. If the Systolic number is a little higher than normal (121 to 139), you have what is called

Prehypertension, and you can usually control it with diet (i.e., less salt) and exercise. If the Systolic number is considerably higher than normal (140 to 159), you have Hypertension Stage One. You will usually get a prescription for medication to control it. If the Systolic number is significantly higher than normal (160 to 179), you now have Hypertension Stage Two. You will undoubtedly get a prescription for stronger medication to control it. However, if the number is extremely higher than normal (e.g., >180), you have reached a Hypertensive Crisis State – immediate emergency care is needed! What can happen? Our heart or arteries can explode! Our bodies are not made to handle such high blood pressure.

The same thing is true about electrical appliances. All appliances work well when the Voltage (electrical pressure) is below 132 Volts. Anything higher is damaging to the appliance. Extremely high electrical pressure (like "Accidental" 240 Volts) can cause an appliance to literally explode. **NOTHING** in your RV is fabricated to operate at such a High Voltage!! At Voltage levels below 132, your electrical appliances will run "contentedly" and probably provide years of excellent service. Operating at variable Voltage levels above 132 Volts will cause progressively cumulative damage that will ultimately result in premature failure (**Comment:** Think of it as the build-up of cholesterol in your heart and arteries – eventually, this build-up could lead to a heart attack or stroke.) When will premature failure occur? Hard to tell. All pieces of equipment react differently to stress, just like people.

Question: What can you do to protect yourself and your RV from High Voltage? One answer is to continuously monitor your incoming Voltage and unplug your RV from shore power as soon as the Voltage is too high. As one of my Electrical

Engineering instructors told me a long time ago, "The best protection is to STOP the problem!"

Minimum **Voltage** requires a little different analogy. For this example, we will again equate it to something else we all understand – a temperate zone. Most of us like to live in a moderate and comfortable climate between 65 and 80 degrees Fahrenheit. When the outside temperature is above 80 degrees, many of us will start looking for an air-conditioned space to stay or work in. When the outside temperature is more than 100 degrees, we curtail outdoor activity. We all know that heat stress leads to heat exhaustion, which can lead to heatstroke – which usually leads to death. Our bodies just do not function well when it's "HOT," and it's obvious, "Heat Kills!"

Again, the same thing is true about electrical appliances. Where does the heat come from? It directly results from the electricity's Current Flow (Amp Draw) through the wiring and appliances. The lower the Voltage, the more Amps it takes to operate an appliance with a Constant Wattage rating. (**Remember:** Our Law of Physics example?) And, the higher the Current Flow, the higher the heat generation. I am sure you have, at one time or another, smelled something electrical, which was "hot" or "burning." The smell was caused by excessively High Current Flow (Amp Draw) and is very distinctive.

For a listing of what Low Voltage (therefore High Current Flow [high heat]) can do to your equipment, you may find the "Cautions Hand-Out for Rallies," one of phred Tinseth's "Poop Sheets," to be highly informative. You can find it at:

manmrk.net/tutorials/RV/phred/surge2.html

So, again, I ask, "What can you do to protect yourself and your RV from Low Voltage, the resulting High Amp Draw, and the possibility of fire?" You could continuously monitor your incoming Voltage and unplug your RV from shore power as soon as the Voltage is too low. "Stop the problem!"

Pause to ponder:
"How do you monitor for High or Low Voltage and unplug when you are away from your RV or sleeping??"

Hmmm..., good question!! But, then, who is going to monitor their incoming Voltage, constantly? There aren't many people who even check the available Voltage at the Post before they plug in. Suppose you are either one of the above. In that case, I have information about an incredibly beneficial product for you later on in this book.

But, first, let's put your new knowledge to a little test. (Don't worry, I'll explain this one as we go along.)

Time to crunch some numbers. So, get out your calculator, a piece of paper, and a pencil or pen, and get ready for a practical scenario.

Note: What follows is a generalized analogy to explain why you <u>must</u> pay attention to the fact you are in an RV and not in your home.

You and your traveling partner are spending a nice weekend in your 50 Amp RV at your favorite campground. It's Sunday morning, and you both have slept in late. You've just finished taking your shower and are about to prepare breakfast while your partner is taking a shower.

First, you turn "ON" the front TV to catch one of those Sunday morning political talk shows. And you decide to put your cell phone on charge because you had a long conversation last night with your sibling (or best friend), and the battery is low.

You open the refrigerator and take out the bread, butter, jam, eggs, bacon, and the coffee container. Nothing like a good breakfast while spending a little time in your RV, enjoying the quiet outdoors.

You prepare the coffee and start the electric pot a-brewing. You put some of the bacon in the microwave and start it cooking – both of you like it crunchy. You begin cooking the eggs on the range top. When it's just the right time, you start the toaster to make your favorite shade of dark brown toast.

Suddenly you notice it starts to get warm in your RV kitchen, so you turn "ON" the air conditioner.

Sounds pretty innocent, doesn't it. It's a routine you have probably done over and over at your home. But, **remember**, you are not in your home; you are in your RV.

A quick, simple mathematical computation will serve to demonstrate how a 50 Amp Service RV can draw a maximum of approximately 100 Amps of current before the Main Breaker "trips." That is, two incoming Lines of 120-Volts with a maximum of 50 Amp draw on each Line. 2L × 120V × 50A equates to a Maximum Wattage capability of 12,000 Watts for the RV (if the Voltage stayed static at 120-Volts).

But, since the Main Breaker will "trip" when just one of the "Hot" Lines reaches 50 Amps, we'll back off 1 Amp on each Line to allow us a minor "fudge factor" (50A – 1A = 49A, and 49A + 49A = 98 Amps). Therefore, 2L × 120V × 49A equates to a safe

Maximum Wattage capability of 11,760 Watts (if the Voltage stayed static at 120-Volts).

For purposes of this example, let us say the Voltage does stay static at 120-Volts. What have you done to your Wattage capacity with all the equipment you innocently turned "ON" and had operating all at the same time?

First, you took a shower. Because you paid for 50 Amp electricity as a part of your campground fee, you're using the electric element in the water heater – that's 1,440 Watts if it's original equipment; 1500 Watts if it was replaced with a typical "house" water heater element. (BTW – not recommended!)

You turned "ON" the HD TV in the living room – 200 Watts.

You plugged in the cell phone charger – 15 Watts.

You opened the absorption refrigerator (runs on LP Gas or Electricity) and had the door open for a while. Now the refrigerator's thermostat has "called for cold." It's running on Auto (electric) – 750 Watts (there are two 375 Watt electric elements) for the "side by side" refrigerator you just had to have because it had more room in it. (*p.s.* the ice maker uses 120 VAC when operating.)

You started the coffee maker – 1,500 Watts.

You started the microwave – 1,400 Watts.

You started the toaster – 1,500 Watts.

You started the air conditioner – 1,800 Watts.

And let's not forget about the converter. All the incandescent lights you have "ON" and all the 12-Volt circuit boards in the water heater, refrigerator, and air conditioner are sucking down quite a bit of 12 VDC. It takes about 480 Watts of AC power for the converter (or inverter/charger) to supply you with that DC power.

When you add up all the Wattage numbers, you get a fantastic total of 9,045 Watts. Is that a lot? Well..., YES, it is!!

You can only use a maximum of the aforementioned 11,760 Watts <u>if</u> the Voltage stayed static at 120-Volts. You are now only 2,715 Watts away from "MAXing out" your RV's power capability. If your partner turns "ON" the latest hairdryer model, add a whopping additional <u>1,875</u> Watts. And then the TV in the bedroom – another 200 Watts. WOW, you are now 640 Watts away from everything shutting down because the breaker on the Post, or your internal Main Breaker, will soon "trip." 11,760W – 640W = 11,120W. 11,120W ÷ 120V = 92.6A. Oh my, you're only 7 Amps away from "tripping" the Main Breaker

In reality, you know the Voltage will not stay static at 120-Volts. (And I know you **remember**, "As Amp Draw goes 'up' [↑], the Voltage goes 'down' [↓]!") How far below the minimum of 104 Volts do you think you have drawn your available Voltage?

Consider this – for every 1,500 Watts of power used, the Voltage drops something like three to four (<u>3</u> to <u>4</u>) Volts. And, if we divide the 9,045W of power usage (re: our practical scenario – pg. 18) by 1,500W, it equates to an equivalent of <u>6</u> <u>M</u>ajor (1,500W) <u>P</u>ieces of <u>E</u>quipment (6-MPE) in operation.

Since 6-MPE × 3V = 18V and 6MPE × 4V = 24V, let's take the middle number (18 + 3 or 24 - 3) between the two products for our example. That's 21 Volts of electrical pressure (Voltage) drop when you run an equivalent of six major appliances simultaneously.

Uh Oh! 120V − 21V = 99V!!!! You are well below the recommended design spec minimum of 104V. (Even if you use the lower example of 18V, you have dropped down to 102V.

Hopefully, a Post or RV Master Breaker had already "tripped" before your Amp Draw got too high, causing the Voltage to go so low. But, what if it didn't? How hot were your wiring and electrical equipment getting? How much damage have <u>you</u> caused to <u>your</u> RV's wiring and electrical equipment just on this leisurely Sunday morning?

Remember, back in the Introduction, where I said, "living in an RV is very different" and "how you must approach electricity "logically" when it applies to RVs," and, also, "House/Commercial electricity usage is one thing, but, using electricity in an RV is something else."

Well, I hope I have gotten my point across with this scenario. You really <u>must</u> pay attention to what you are doing when you live in an RV − even if it's just for the weekend.

And what about those of you traveling from Point A to Destination B and own a 50 Amp RV but do not want to pay the extra $2 or $3 for the 50 Amp power at an overnight campground? If you limit yourself to 30 Amps, your Maximum Wattage capability is a mere 3,600 Watts (120V × 30A = 3,600W)! That is a significant change from 12,000 Watts. In fact, it is a **<u>70% drop</u>** in Total Wattage capability − a real substantial difference between "just existing" and "living comfortably" in your 50 Amp RV!! And what about the damage you are causing to your Plug Head, Power Cord, and appliances by overdrawing Current Flow past the weakened 30 Amp breaker at the Post. Are you really saving something, or will you ultimately be sacrificing more? (You may recall the old Fram Filter commercial which said, "Pay me now, or pay me later!")

Okay..., now, let's move on to **Circuit Breakers.**

As mentioned earlier, a Circuit Breaker is a safety device. A Circuit Breaker is always located at the beginning of a wire run – close to where the Voltage is first applied to the wire – i.e., the source. (**Remember** the previous comment about using a water pressure regulator?) Hopefully, there is a Circuit Breaker at the Post where you plug in. It should be there to protect your Plug Head and Power Cord. Just inside the RV, close to where the Power Cord terminates, is your Power Distribution Panel. This panel distributes electrical pressure throughout the RV. The Circuit Breakers mounted inside this panel are there to protect all the 120 VAC wiring and equipment inside your RV. (**Sidebar:** Most RVs use automotive, blade-type fuses to protect the 12 VDC systems.)

A Circuit Breaker "opens" (switches "OFF") to prevent the wire from overheating from too high of a Current Flow (Amp Draw). **WARNING:** If the wire gets too hot, it can start a fire!!

How does it work since there is no ammeter (a special tool that electronically "reads" and numerically displays Amps) attached to a Circuit Breaker? Metaphorically, there is a "spring" under the switch inside the breaker. When you turn the breaker "ON," the "spring" is compressed. Current passes through the spring as a part of the flow path. Each "spring" has a rated tensile strength. When it is heated by the Current Flow passing through it, it will expand. When the expansion reaches its maximum design spec, the "spring" will "trip" the breaker open ("OFF").

Although we use breakers at the Post as "ON/OFF" switches, they were never designed for such a function. Think about what happens to a piece of metal when you bend it back and forth repeatedly. Right! – It gets weak/brittle and ultimately breaks.

The same sort of thing happens to Circuit Breakers when they are opened and closed repeatedly. They wear out and fail to function correctly. A weakened "spring" cannot push the switch "OFF" at the proper current (heat) level, resulting in more Current Flow than the wire attached to the breaker is designed for. (*Gee – maybe that's one of the reasons so many Plug Heads on 30 Amp Power Cords and Adapters get burnt-out or melted!!*)

(**Recommendation:** Even though a Circuit Breaker was never designed to be a switch, USE IT if it is there! Always shut the breaker "OFF" before you plug in and shut it "OFF" again before removing your Power Cord's Plug Head from the Post's Outlet. Protect yourself from a deadly electrical shock!!)

A 50 Amp RV plugged into a 30 Amp Outlet can easily overdraw current beyond a weakened breaker's capacity. (**Comment:** My wife and I full-timed in a 50 Amp RV. We only used a 30 Amp Outlet when a 50 was not available. And when adapted "down" to 30 Amps, we were very cautious about how much equipment we turned "ON" and how many total Amps we were drawing past the breaker on the Post.)

WARNING: If you have a 30 Amp RV, you cannot run more equipment just because you're adapted up to a 50 Amp Outlet (and many people, unbelievably, think they can)! Your RV's wiring can't handle the additional Current Flow. If you have a 30 Amp RV and must adapt "up" to a 50 Amp Outlet, be very aware – you do **not** have a 30 Amp breaker at the Post to protect your Power Cord or your RV and equipment!! Because you have an oversized 50 Amp breaker protecting your plug-in Outlet, you can overdraw your maximum Current Flow level very quickly. Be extremely careful if you adapt "up" – the potential for fire increases dramatically!!

(**Comment:** Constant use wears out Circuit Breakers and Outlets mounted at the Post. In my humble opinion, all campgrounds should replace every breaker and Outlet, at least once every five years – maybe even earlier. Unfortunately, I have not run across any campgrounds or RV parks practicing a regular or rotational replacement program. [See Appendix # 1 for important information.]

In defense of the campground owners, they are not responsible for High or Low Voltage – the electric companies are [they are the ones who make and distribute the electricity]. The campground owner is only responsible for providing a safe and efficient electrical path for the Voltage [electrical pressure] to be made available for your RV.

And never forget – It is considered an invasion of private property if you do anything to the campground's Outlet box on the Post, other than plugging in and unplugging your Power Cord. If you think you have a problem at the Post, notify the campground's management office. [**Remember:** A safe RVer is a considerate and law-abiding RVer.])

RV Wiring Differences

Each RV is wired explicitly for a particular Amp Service – 50A <u>or</u> 30A. It is one or the other, **not both**. Each RV has a fixed amount of wiring and equipment based on its designed Amp Service capability. An RV wired for 50 Amp Service can adapt "down" to the 30 Amp Outlet at the Post. And an RV wired for 30 Amp Service can adapt "up" to a 50 Amp Outlet at the Post. Wired explicitly <u>for a particular Amp Service</u> and <u>the capability to adapt "up" or "down"</u> are **two totally different concepts**.

The RV Power Cords are explicitly manufactured for a specific Amp Service, as evidenced in the following photo.

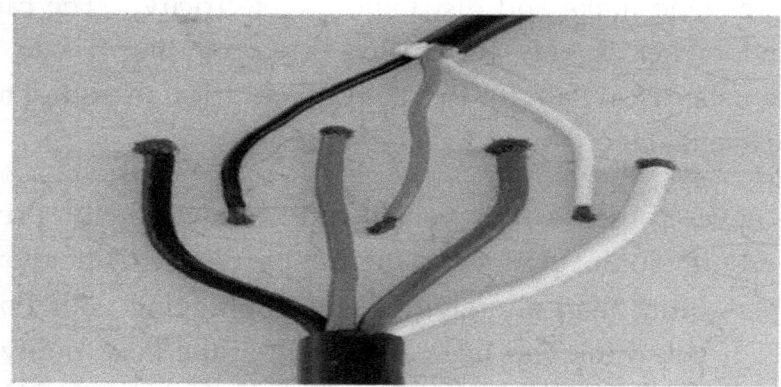

Top set of Wires – 30 Amp Power Cord, Three - 10 AWG Wires. (Black, Green, and White)

Bottom set of Wires – 50 Amp Power Cord, Three - 6 AWG Wires. (Black, Red, and White), and One - 8 AWG Wire (Green).

Note: The smaller the AWG (American Wire Gauge) number, the larger the wire.

30 AMP RV – One (1) Line of incoming 120-Volts: maximum 30 Amp draw.

Black - Hot Wire (Electrical Pressure from the Grid)
White - Neutral Wire (Return Path to the Grid)
Green - Ground Wire (Safety Back Door/Exit to the Grid)

Possible Wiring Faults for 30 Amp RVs:

Accidental 240V – The Outlet is <u>incorrectly</u> wired (i.e., as if it were a Dryer or Oven Outlet), resulting in 240-Volts entering the RV via what should be the Hot (in) and Neutral (out) Lines, but, now, two Hots are coming in (120 + 120 = 240). As stated earlier, absolutely **none** of the equipments in your RV equipment is designed to operate at this High Voltage level! *Instantly destructive.*

Reverse Polarity – the Hot and Neutral Wires are connected backward. (Black to the normal White connection and White to the normal Black connection.) The flow of electricity is reversed. Ground Fault Circuit Interrupt (GFCI) Safety Outlets will <u>not</u> function with Reverse Polarity – they "trip" immediately! Also, the Circuit Breakers at the RV's panel box are ineffective because the electricity is getting to the equipment via the Neutral Wire path, not the Hot Wire path – meaning backward! Even if the Circuit Breaker is turned "OFF," the equipment is still energized – a constant shock hazard!! An overload might trip the breaker, but the wiring and appliances are unprotected from High Amp Draw since the breaker is now on the Neutral side. The excess current could continue to flow until the circuit <u>burns</u> "open." *Fire is the likely conse-quence.*

Open Ground – The Ground Wire is not connected. Therefore, there is no "Emergency Exit or Back Door" for errant electricity. (**Comment:** If a piece of equipment or appliance Shorts to Ground [a.k.a. crashes internally], the Voltage will follow the attached Ground Wire to return to the grid.) The Ground Wire is **NOT** a normal path for electricity (hence, the term: "errant [somewhere it doesn't belong] electricity"). An Open Ground can result in a "hot skin" shock hazard (i.e., Voltage running through the chassis and metal structure of the RV). *This condition could be "shockingly" deadly!!*

Open Neutral – The Neutral (White) wire is not connected, or its circuit is "open." Consequently, there is no "return path" to the grid for the electricity. This could result in arcing and a potentially deadly shock hazard. None of your equipment will work unless Shorted to Ground - *An unnatural condition*.

Conceptually, an RV wired for 30 Amp Service has one (1) Line of 120 VAC, which provides electrical pressure (Voltage) to all the RV appliances and outlets.

At the Power Distribution Panel, each appliance has its own secondary wiring from the Main Power Line. This wiring is routed through separate Circuit Breakers (20 or 15 Amp) for additional protection.

However, there is still just one Line of electricity coming to the RV; accordingly, there is only one 30 Amp breaker at the Power Distribution Panel. This breaker is referred to as the RV's "Main Breaker."

(Conceptual Image)

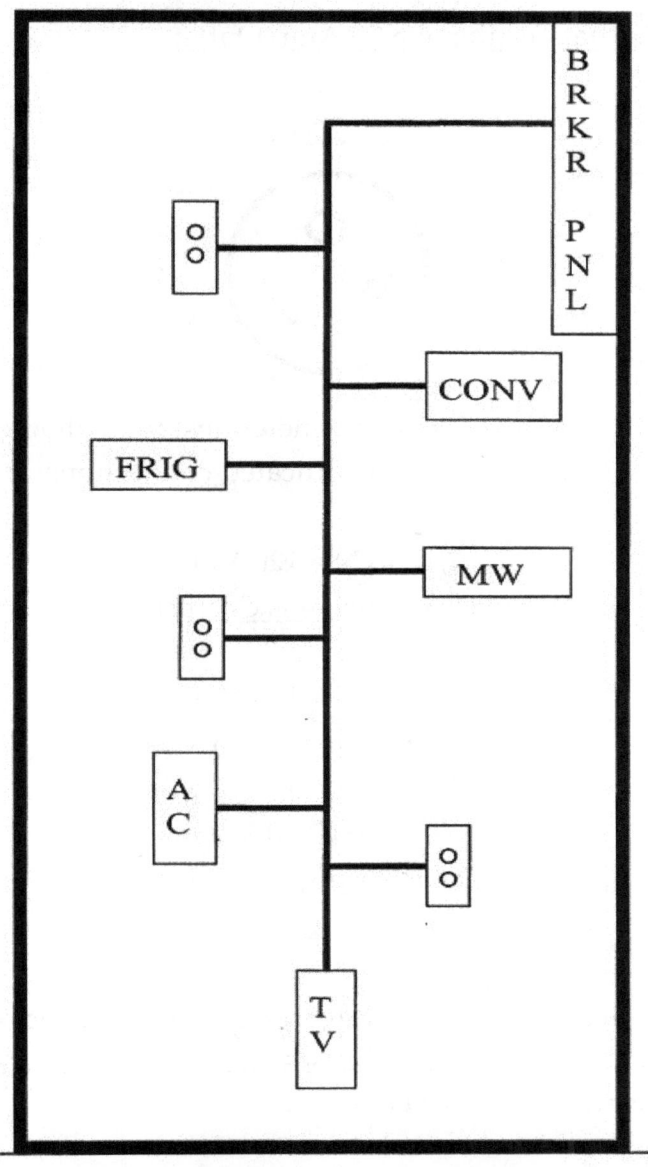

30 AMP RV ELECTRICAL SERVICE
One (1) line of 120 volts
Maximum 30 amp draw

Initial Manual Testing of a 30 Amp Outlet

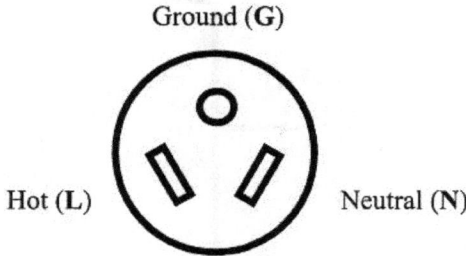

Using a handheld voltmeter, test for Voltages by "probing" the indicated connections:

If, L to N ≈ 120-Volts,
Then: Wiring is Correct.

If, L to G ≈ 120-Volts,
Then: Wiring is Correct.

If, N to G = 0 Volts,
Then: Wiring is Correct.

Note: The symbol "≈" is a mathematical expression for "Approximately Equal To" (i.e., 120 or 240 Volts, ± 2 or 3 Volts. A Voltage reading will not always be exactly 120 or 240 Volts.)

And here are some "**DO NOT PLUG-IN**" FAULTS to test for:

If, N to G ≈ 120-Volts,
And, L to G = 0 Volts,
Then: Reverse Polarity exists at the Outlet.

If, L to N = 0 Volts,
And, L to G ≈ 120-Volts,
Then: Open Neutral exists at the Outlet.

If, L to N ≈ 120-Volts,
And, L to G = 0 Volts,
Then: Open Ground exists at the Outlet.

If, L to N > 132 Volts,
Then: High Voltage exists at the Outlet.

If, L to N < 104 Volts,
Then: Low Voltage exists at the Outlet.

If, L to N ≈ 240 Volts,
Then: the Outlet is **NOT** wired for any RV!

50 AMP RV – Two (2) Lines of incoming 120-Volts: maximum 50 Amp draw *on each Line*.

Black – Hot Wire # 1
Red – Hot Wire # 2 (This second Line of incoming Voltage is a significant difference!!)
White – Neutral Wire
Green – Ground Wire

Possible Wiring Faults for 50 Amp RVs:

Accidental 240V – The two Hot Wires are connected, resulting in 240 Volts entering the RV on both Lines (120 + 120 = 240). As stated earlier, absolutely **none** of the equipments in your RV equipment is designed to operate at this High Voltage level! *Instantly destructive.*

Reverse Polarity – Exactly the same as on a 30 Amp RV, **but** one (1) of the Hot Wires and the Neutral Wire are connected backward. This means the miswired Hot is now connected to the "return path." This **will** result in Accidental 240V when a unit of equipment is turned "ON" at the other Hot side of the RV! (120V from the normally wired Hot will intersect with the 120V from the Hot wired to the Neutral side.) *Instantly destructive and a shock hazard.*

WARNING: "Adapting" down to use a 15 Amp, three-light tester (a.k.a. Polarity Checker) will **only** allow you to check Line 1 for Reverse Polarity. The Polarity of Line 2 **cannot** be checked this way!! Because of this Line 2 "blind spot," testing in this manner prevents you from **completely** detecting a damaging Reverse Polarity Fault at a 50 Amp Outlet.

Open Ground – Exactly the same as on a 30 Amp RV.

Open Neutral – The same as on a 30 Amp RV, the Neutral (White) wire is not connected. Hence, there is no "return path" for electricity. This can result in a deadly shock hazard. However, <u>**unlike the 30 Amp RV**</u>, it <u>**will**</u> result in Accidental 240V because the <u>Higher Voltage</u> on the <u>Low Amp Line</u> (A↓ ∴ V↑) will intersect with the <u>Lower Voltage</u> on the <u>High Amp Line</u> (A↑ ∴ V↓) as it forces its way past to get out. This all means that the Hot Line with the Highest Amp Draw or load (therefore, Lowest Voltage) will be **forced** to become the Neutral (return) path – another Law of Physics. And, yes, electricity <u>can</u> run two directions at the same time on the same piece of wire [i.e., Out-of-Phase Voltage (more about this later)].) *Instantly destructive – usually to all the equipment attached to the Hot Line in the RV to which your inverter/converter is connected (including the inverter/converter).* (**Comment:** Every time your RV is plugged into shore power, the inverter/converter typically has an immediate High Amp Draw - it always starts in Bulk (High Amp Output) Mode.)

Note: The symbol ∴ (used above) is a mathematical and shorthand expression for "thus" or "therefore."

Conceptually, an RV wired for 50 Amp Service has two separate Lines of 120 VAC. Each Line provides electrical pressure (Voltage) to one-half (1/2) of the appliances and Outlets within the RV.

Starting at the power company's transformer (it looks like a large trash can near the top of the electric pole), which supplies ("feeds") electricity to the campground, all the way to the Outlet at your Post, these two Lines stay apart from one another. THEY NEVER TOUCH!! Through the Power Cord and at the Power Distribution Panel inside the RV, they always remain separated. (**Remember:** Accidental 240V if they don't!)

When your RV was designed, the engineers attempted to balance the electrical load. To do this, each Line of 120 VAC in the RV has a specific amount of Wattage capable equipment attached to it (approximately 6,000 Watts). When all the RV's appliances are turned "ON" simultaneously, they will draw a nearly equal amount of current on their respective Lines – with a maximum of 50 Amps per Line. (**Remember:** Our Laws of Physics and Mathematics!)

Each appliance in a 50 Amp RV also has its own secondary wiring routed through a separate Circuit Breaker (20 or 15 Amp) for additional protection. The Outlets throughout the 50 Amp RV are usually split with half on one breaker and half on another breaker.

(See Appendix # 3 for information about "Labeling Hot Lines and Outlets" in a 50 Amp RV.)

(Conceptual Image)

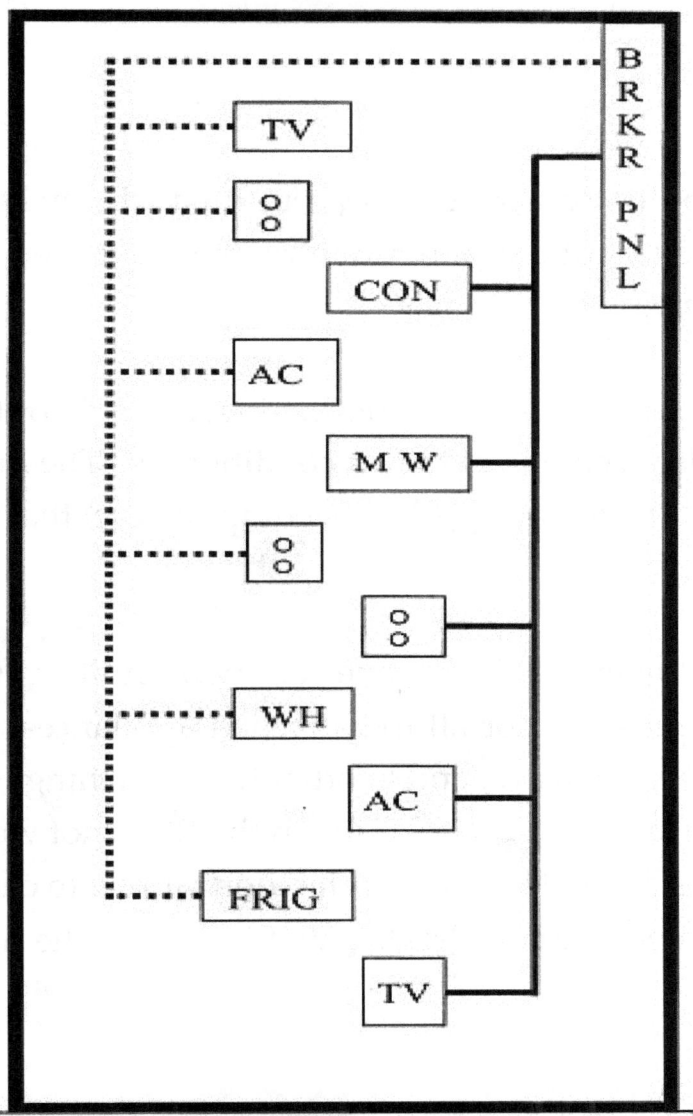

50 AMP RV ELECTRICAL SERVICE WITH A CONVERTER
Two (2) lines of incoming 120 volts
Maximum 50 amp draw *on each line*
(100 Amps Total)

Conceptually, a 50 Amp RV, outfitted with an Inverter, is wired a little differently than one equipped with a Converter.

The 120 VAC Line feeding the inverter side of the RV will also feed one of the air conditioners. The inverter, in turn, feeds the appliances/equipment on that particular Line.

Most inverters have one or two built-in Circuit Breakers – one for all the attached appliances, or one for the microwave, and another for everything else fed by the inverter. If something in the RV is not working, and is supplied by the inverter, don't forget to check for a "tripped" Circuit Breaker that is part of the inverter itself.

(Conceptual Image)

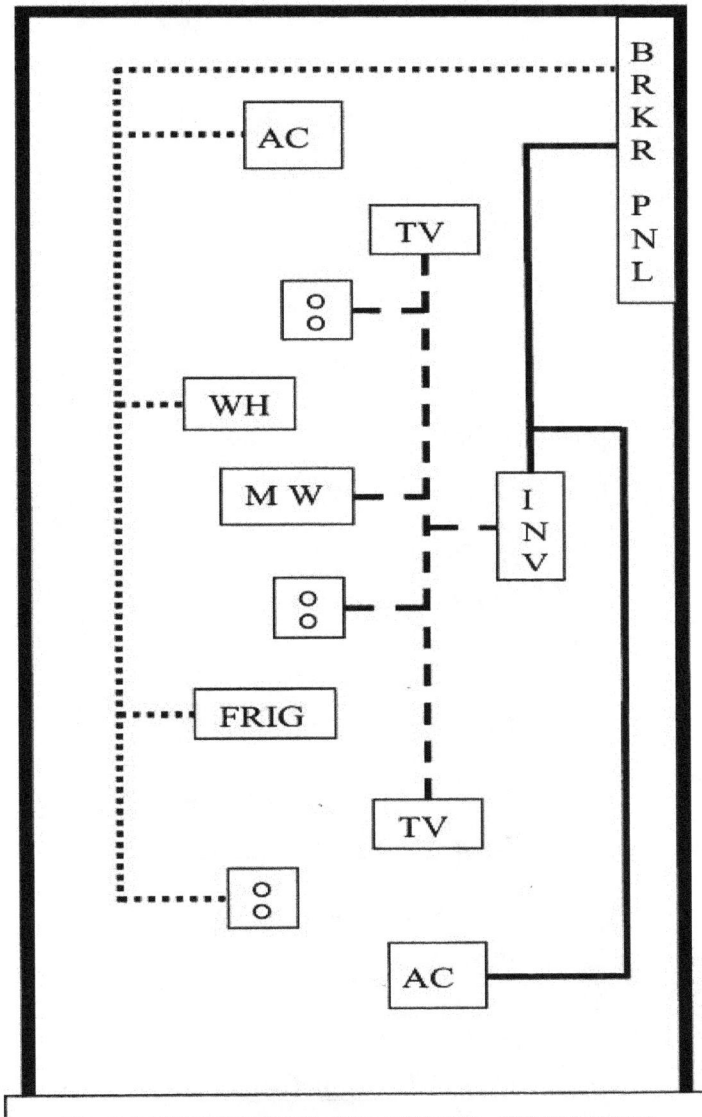

50 AMP RV ELECTRICAL SERVICE WITH AN INVERTER
Two (2) lines of incoming 120 volts
Maximum 50 amp draw *on each line*
(100 Amps Total)

Initial Manual Testing of a 50 Amp Outlet

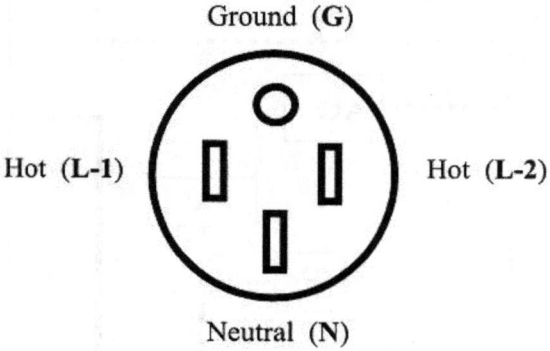

Using a handheld voltmeter, test for Voltages by "probing" the indicated connections:

If, L-1 to N ≈ 120-Volts,
Then: Wiring is Correct.

If, L-2 to N ≈ 120-Volts,
Then: Wiring is Correct.

If, L-1 to L-2 ≈ 240 Volts,
Then: Wiring is Correct.

If, N to G = 0 Volts,
Then: Wiring is Correct.

If, L-1 to G ≈ 120-Volts,
Then: Wiring is Correct.

If, L-2 to G ≈ 120-Volts,
Then: Wiring is Correct.

And here are some "**DO NOT PLUG-IN**" FAULTS to test for:

If N to G ≈ 120-Volts,
Then: Reverse Polarity exists at the Outlet,
AND, If L-1 to G = 0 Volts,
Then: Reverse Polarity is on L-1.
OR, If L-2 to G = 0 Volts,
Then: Reverse Polarity is on L-2.

If L-1 to N = 0 Volts and/or L-2 to N = 0 Volts,
AND L-1 to G ≈ 120-Volts and L-2 to G ≈ 120-Volts,
Then: Open Neutral exists at the Outlet.

If L-1 to N ≈ 120-Volts and/or L-2 to N ≈ 120-Volts,
AND L-1 to G = 0 Volts and L-2 to G = 0 Volts,
Then: Open Ground exists at the Outlet.

If L-1 or L-2 to N > 132 Volts,
Then: High Voltage exists at the Outlet.

If L-1 or L-2 to N < 104 Volts,
Then: Low Voltage exists at the Outlet.

If L-1 and/or L-2 to N ≈ 240 Volts,
Then: the Outlet is **NOT** wired for any RV!

Also, it is a good idea to test for the following:

If, Adapted "down" from 50 Amp Service to a 30 Amp Outlet,
And, L-1 to L-2 = 0 Volts (YES, <u>zero</u>!),
Then: <u>Wiring is Correct</u>.

(**Note:** This last "test" can only be performed at the 30M to 50F adapter's female end.)

<u>**WARNING**</u>**:** If the Outlet you intend to use at the Post (30 Amp or 50 Amp) is wired correctly, the initial testing methodology described will <u>only</u> provide you with "preliminary" Voltage readings. The operating Voltages **<u>will</u> <u>change</u>** after you remove your probes, plug in your RV's Power Cord, and apply any type of load to the electrical source (turn something "ON"). <u>GUARANTEED</u>!

(**Comment:** The Whole RV, Electrical Protection Units discussed later in this book will make all the aforementioned Outlet checks automatically and will not allow a Wiring Fault to cause costly damage to your RV's 120-Volt wiring and equipment. Furthermore, they will monitor and protect your RV from damage caused by high or low incoming Voltage, as well as the ever feared "surge.")

50 Amp Power Distribution Panel
Copyright © 2010 by Dale Lee Sumner
SUMDALUS-USA

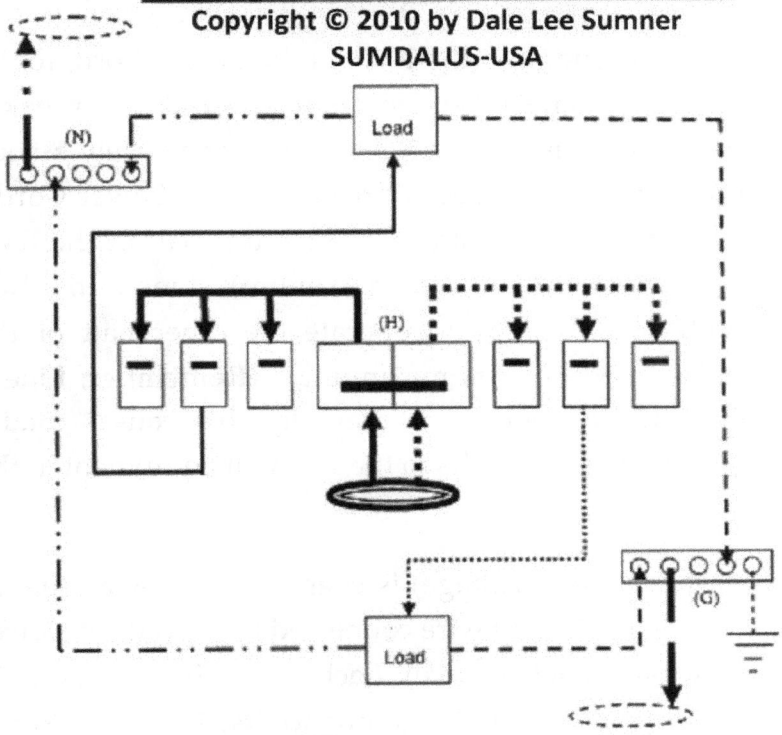

LEGEND:

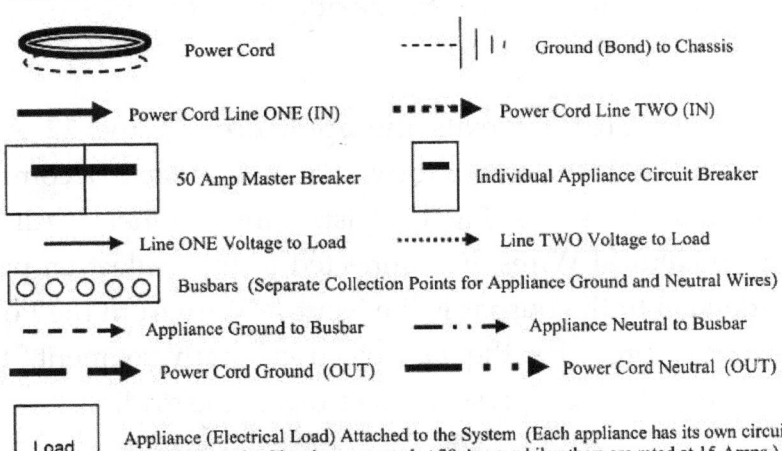

39

The Normal Path for 50 Amp Service Voltage

It comes from the grid, into the RV, via the Power Cord, to the Power Distribution Panel (also referred to as the Circuit Breaker Panel). From here, it is distributed to the appropriately associated Circuit Breakers. Voltage sourced from the Power Cord's Line 1 (the Black wire) is used to operate one-half of the RV's electrical equipment (6,000 Watts maximum). Line 2 (the Red wire) provides the Voltage to operate the other half of the equipment (also 6,000 Watts maximum). (**Remember:** Line 1 and Line 2 NEVER touch – if they do, this causes totally damaging Accidental 240 Volts to the 120-Volt equipment in the RV!)

The electrical pressure (Voltage) is channeled to the appliance via a 12 AWG "Hot" (black) wire connected to the <u>output</u> side of the Circuit Breaker (safety device). Each Circuit Breaker protects the wiring attached to it and the appliance itself from excessive Current Flow (High Amp Draw). The sourced electrical pressure is used to run/operate the attached appliance when its on/off switch is turned "ON."

The electrical pressure exits the appliance via the 12 AWG Neutral (White) Wire, which forwards the Voltage to a common busbar located at the Power Distribution Panel. All the appliance Neutral Wires are connected to this collection point. Also attached to the busbar is the Neutral Wire from the Power Cord. This provides the last electrical path segment, thus allowing the electrical pressure to return to the grid.

A 12 AWG Ground Wire is likewise attached to each appliance. This wire provides a separate path for "errant" Voltage to escape from a failed/crashed/shorted appliance back to a different busbar, also located in the Power Distribution Panel. The Ground busbar is distinctively attached to the chassis by a stand-alone Ground (bonding) Wire. In addition, the Ground Wire from the Power Cord is attached to the busbar. This completes the path for any "Errant" Voltage to flow out of the RV, back to the grid's grounding rod.

Note: The two busbars are physically and electrically isolated from each other to ensure the Neutral and Ground Wires never come in contact with one another. (**Remember:** "Hot Skin" (electrically charged chassis), and possibly electrocution, if they do!)

(**Comment:** The 30 Amp Power Distribution Panel is similar, but with three differences: **1**. There is NO Line 2. **2**. The Master Breaker is a single 30 Amp device, and, **3**. 3,600 Watts maximum.)

LEGEND: (For all Busbar Examples on the following pages.)

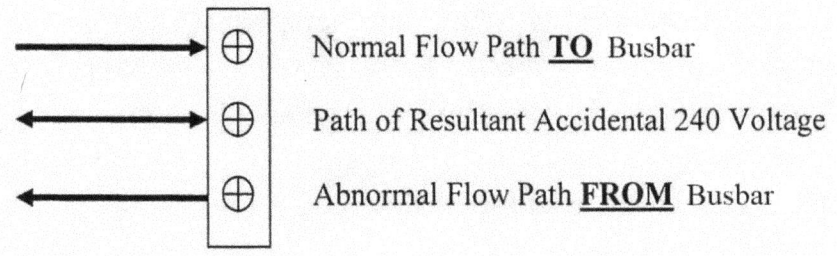

Normal Flow Path **TO** Busbar

Path of Resultant Accidental 240 Voltage

Abnormal Flow Path **FROM** Busbar

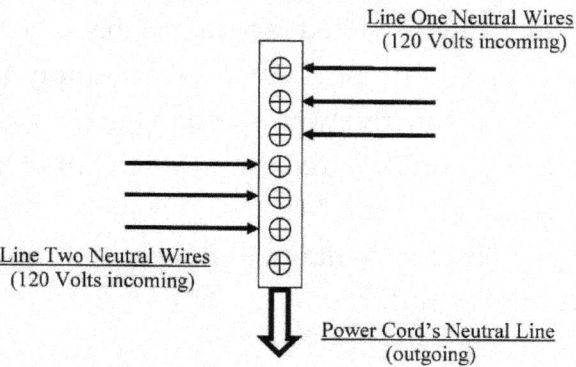

Aside from Accidental 240 Volts, any Wiring Fault, which affects the 50 Amp Neutral Busbar, will be the <u>most damaging</u> event that could happen to any RV. Three such events are possible:

1. **Reverse Polarity** will result in the loss of at least one-half of the RV's 120-Volt equipment. The side affected will be the side opposite the Reverse Polarity.

2. **Open Neutral** will also result in losing at least one-half of the RV's 120-Volt equipment. The side affected will typically be the side the converter or inverter/charger is attached to.

3. A **Loose Neutral** will have the same effect as Open Neutral once a heavy load is applied to the system. (e.g., No problem(s) evident until the battery "bulk charge/equalizing" mode or any other High Wattage item starts operating, causing an extremely High Amp Draw to be established.)

(**Comment**: Because these Wiring Faults are so devastating when they occur, they are quite often, <u>and incorrectly</u>, believed to be the ever-feared SURGE when, in fact, they are **not**. A Surge does not occur too often, but Wiring Faults do!)

Reverse Polarity Affect at the 50 Amp Neutral Busbar

Line One and Neutral Crossed = Resultant 240V on Line Two
(Just the opposite occurs if Line Two and Neutral are crossed.)

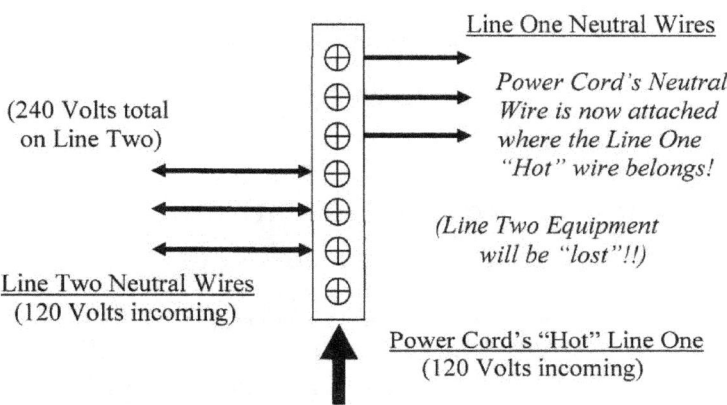

Open Neutral Affect at the 50 Amp Neutral Busbar

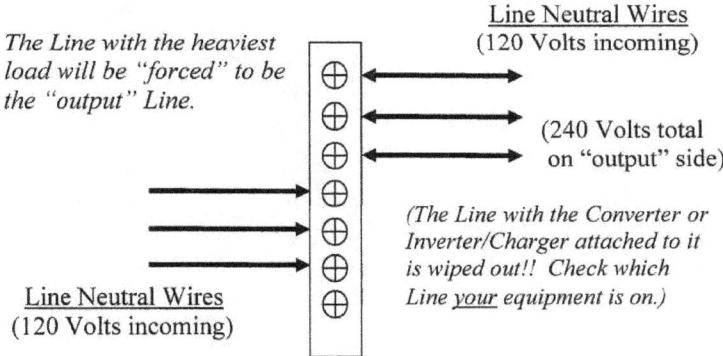

The Line with the most substantial Amp Draw will have the lowest Voltage and will be the Line forced to be the "output" (Neutral) to the grid – resulting in 240 Volts on the "output" Line. Typically, the Line the Converter or Inverter/Charger is attached to will have the heaviest load when the RV is initially plugged in. (The Converter or Charger is always "ON" to provide 12 VDC battery charging – initially at a maximum AC Amp Draw.)

Whether your RV is wired for 30 or 50 Amp Service, by now, you, obviously, realize the most dangerous thing you do while RVing is, "*Plug into the Post.*" The Post is the most susceptible location for unintended connection errors when it comes to Wiring Faults!

Suppose an electrical problem exists at your RV's "point of connection" to the electrical grid. In that case, this chart approximates the probability of occurrence (out of 100%):

Possible Problem	Campground Post	Rally Field Generator
Accidental 240 Volts	5 %	5 %
Reverse Polarity	25 %	15 %
Open Neutral	25 %	15 %
Open Ground	10 %	15 %
Voltage Surge / Spike	5 %	15 %
High Voltage	5 %	35 % **
Low Voltage	25 % *	< 1 %
High Frequency (Cycles)	< 1 %	< 1 %
Low Frequency (Cycles)	< 1 %	< 1 %

The *highlighted* electrical problems **WILL** cause immediate and catastrophic damage to some or all of your RV's equipment!

Note: *As stated before, High and Low Voltage problems will cause unpredictable but cumulative damage and, subsequently, premature failure – think of it to be similar to the build-up of cholesterol in your heart and arteries – ultimately, this build-up could lead to a "heart attack."*

* This percentage will be much higher when large crowds are present at a campground on holiday weekends. (**Remember:** When the Amp Draw goes "up" [equipment turned "ON"], the Voltage goes "down.")

** Field generators are typically operated at High Output Voltage levels because of anticipated High Amp Draw. However, after sunset, as connected users turn "OFF" equipment, the generator output is NOT automatically adjusted downward. The higher the generator's starting Output Voltage without a load, the higher the percentage.

Surge

This one word gets knocked around the old campground/RV park quite a bit. Maybe it's time to explain what it is and what it is not.

An actual surge is an unusual case of Extremely High Voltage (hundreds of Volts) raging through the electrical grid like a supersonic jet – it is fast and furious. As quickly as it hits, "BOOM," it's gone. It could be caused by lightning or by failed power company equipment. Whichever the cause, it is very damaging to an RV!

However, contrary to popular belief, a surge is not the big bugaboo everyone thinks it is. It is, in fact, the **least** common problem for RVs! Yes, <u>it could be very damaging if it occurs</u>, but it only happens 1% or 5% of the time.

    1% – if the electric company cannot contain a surge generated from within their system.

    5% – if it came from good 'ole Mother Nature – yep, lightning strikes.

(**Comment:** There is only a slim chance you, personally, or your RV, specifically, might be struck by lightning during any one year [the odds are something like 1 in 700,000 or more – but, the longer you live, or the longer/more you RV, the odds get slightly lower]. However, despite this sort of probability, you should check out Canada's Environment and Climate Change website:

canada.ca/en/environment-climate-change.
(search for "lightning safety when camping")

This site contains important information about lightning safety for Camp Trailers and RVs. They may help you prevent any significant problems from occurring while using an RV when a lightning storm is threatening your location.)

One thing is for sure, if an actual electrical surge finds your campground's/park's underground grid, it will affect <u>EVERY RV</u> plugged in on the same grid or electrical path!! However, if you, or maybe a neighbor, were the only one who got "hit" in your occupied park…it certainly **was not** a surge. Stop a second and think about a hurricane surge – it hits everyone and everything in its path, not just one or two here and there, like a tornado. Well, an electrical surge hits everyone, too!!

(**Another Comment:** Although an actual surge occurs very infrequently, I speak from experience when I say, "Surge Suppression is a good thing to have." Our RV was indirectly "attacked" by lightning when we were at the FMCA Rally at Concord, NC, in 2006. A powerful electrical storm rolled in one night and played havoc in the area for over two hours. The field generator from which we were receiving shore power was directly hit by lightning. An actual surge went out through its output power cables. Fortunately, our RV had surge suppression as an integral part of a 120-Volt, Whole RV, Electrical Protection Unit. [More about this type of device will be discussed later in this book.] Other than a "blown" [a.k.a. dead] surge module, we did not sustain any other damage, and believe me, as an RV tech with all the nifty electrical testing tools, I checked. Unfortunately, I cannot say my three neighbors were so lucky. They <u>each</u> sustained between $2,000 and $8,000 worth of damage to their internal electrical equipment and RV wiring system.)

There are seven or eight inexpensive models of "Surge (ONLY) Protectors" on the market. These units have just one truly protective feature – they provide "Surge Suppression" – often in a limited amount. True, they may have some Wiring Fault diagnostic capability and identify any discovered Faults via small lights or LEDs. However, this diagnostic capability is NOT automatic protection. You must interpret what the lights are "telling" you and take appropriate action yourself – you must physically unplug from the Post. **Note:** None of the "surge-only" units can detect any Voltage problems, nor can most of them "tell" you if the surge module is dead! If you are going to buy any type of "surge protector," please make sure the unit you are considering can let you know if the internal surge suppression module has failed and is no longer effective. WHY? Because all RV surge suppression systems sacrifice their "lives" to protect you and your equipment. It might be a quick death from a lightning strike or a slow death from repeated High (Transient) Voltage spikes coming from the power company. How do you know if that "surge thing" between your RV and the Post is doing you any good?

If you or your neighbor had been the "only one who got hit" on the row, and the "hit" did not occur when you first plugged in, it was probably caused by something I refer to as an **IED** (**I**nadvertent **E**lectrical **D**isruption).

The damage to electrical equipment/systems from an IED "hit" is usually the consequence of someone (let's pray it wasn't you) unintentionally interfering with the shore power system. A few examples are provided here, and there are, indeed, more possibilities:

1. Accidently crushing or separating power supply connections. Please, do not drive over anyone's Power Cord or any type of power supply wires lying on the ground. While an RV Power

Cord's internal wiring can be crushed together or broken, a rally field generator's output power cables have "snap-together" connections that can be easily separated. (**Remember:** What happens to a 50 Amp RV if the Neutral Wire/Cable is not connected [a.k.a. open], or the two Hot Lines are fused together.)

2. Starting an onboard generator when an RV's Power Cord has not been physically removed from the shore power system, first. **NEVER** start a generator without completely disconnecting your Power Cord from the Post (do not just trip the breaker). Do not blindly expect an automatic transfer switch (ATS) to always protect your RV from two electrical power sources simultaneously. (**Comment:** Think in terms of Accidental 240V! A frequent cause – RV owners "exercising" their generators while still plugged into shore power!)

3. Plugging into the Post with flawed power Adapters or damaged Power Cord Plug Heads.

(**Advice:** If your Adapter, Power Cord, or Plug Head is faulty in any way [e.g., tine(s) charred, rubber/plastic around any tine is melted, the cable's rubber casing is separated from the Plug Head, or the exterior sheathing cut/severed] – do not ignore it or just apply a "band-aid" fix! **REPLACE** the dangerous piece as soon as you can. It's not worth the potential damage it can cause if you continue to use it!!)

(**Comment:** One of my Dad's constant "counselings" to my brother and me when we were teenagers certainly seems to be applicable here: "HEY! Pay attention to what you're doing!" Any type of IED is, unfortunately, a frequent cause of costly damage to RVs. And, I'm referring to the potential damage of wiping out all of your 120 VAC appliances/equipment, too.)

Here's a motto from Mobile RV Medic, Inc. that my wife coined, and I recommend you pay particular attention to:

"When it comes to RVs and damaging outside electricity, ignorance isn't bliss, my friends – it's expensive!"

IMPORTANT WARNINGS

1. **WARNING:** Unlike house wiring, the RV's Ground and Neutral Wires should **NEVER** – **NEVER** – **NEVER** be tied/bonded together! This will result in an immediate "hot skin" shock hazard that could be deadly. (**Remember:** Ground and Neutral Wires each have their own busbars – physically and electrically isolated from each other.) (See Appendix # 4 for critically important information.)

2. **ANOTHER WARNING:** If you decide to have a 30 or 50 Amp electrical Outlet installed at your home for your RV, be extraordinarily careful!! A "house" electrician will look at the Outlet and assume it is a 240 Volt Outlet (like a dryer or oven Outlet) and wire it accordingly. Make sure you tell him (or her), "It's one Line (or two Lines for 50 Amp) of 120-Volts – NOT 240!!"

3. **SPECIAL WARNING:** DON'T EVEN THINK ABOUT self-installing a 240 Volt appliance in your RV (e.g., clothes dryer)!! It's too damn dangerous. PERIOD!

Converter or Inverter???

Are you confused as to whether you have a Converter or an Inverter in your RV? Maybe the following will help solve the mystery.

A **CONVERTER** is an electrical component which "Converts" (changes) 120-Volts of Alternating Current into 12-Volts of Direct Current. Let's use a simple phrase to help remember what a converter does. Think of it this way:

A **C**onverter takes 120 V**A**C and "lowers" it to 12 V**D**C."
Written graphically as C » A ↓ D, or just **C A D** for short.

The converter can be located anywhere inside the RV. It is always plugged into a 120 VAC Outlet. It provides 12 VDC to the equipment/components attached to the 12-Volt wiring system via the battery system and a fuse panel. The 12 VDC components include the furnace, water heater, refrigerator, thermostat, TV antenna, and most interior RV lights. The converter also provides a charging capability to maintain the battery/ies (trickle charge or three-stage charging). Not surprisingly, the converter only works when you are plugged into shore power or running your generator.

An **INVERTER** is an electrical component which "Inverts" (a different type of change) 12-Volts of Direct Current into 120-Volts of Alternating Current (just the opposite of the converter). Here's another simple phrase to remember what an inverter does:

An **I**nverter takes 12 V**D**C and "raises" it to 120 V**A**C."
Written graphically as I » D ↑ A, or just **I D A** for short.

The inverter is usually in a basement compartment, close to the battery bank known as the "house" battery/ies. It receives power from one of two sources.

1. When plugged into shore power, the inverter receives its power from the Power Distribution Panel (120 VAC). It is usually via its own 30 Amp Circuit Breaker. Unbeknownst to most, the inverter has its own unique automatic transfer switch (ATS) built into the unit. When the ATS recognizes it is receiving shore power (secondary source), the incoming power is just "passed through" the inverter to the attached appliances (typically the microwave, television(s), and a select number of Outlets). A small amount of 120 VAC is used to run the "charger" side of the inverter. This charger maintains the battery/ies just like a converter, and it, too, usually <u>cannot</u> be turned "OFF."

2. When you **are not** plugged into shore power or running your generator, the inverter's ATS switches direction. Now it receives its power from the "house" battery bank (primary source) and does its inversion magic to provide 120 VAC power to the attached appliances. Sorry to say so, but contrary to common thought, when the inverter is working on battery power, it does <u>not</u> run its "charger" side to recharge the battery/ies.

Hopefully, the basic explanations above will enable you to decide if your RV is a **CAD** or an **IDA**. (For more in-depth information about converters and inverters, please read our *Primer* titled, *Understanding Your RV's "BATTERY POWER" – 12-Volt Electricity.*)

Here are some quick remarks about **Autoformers.**

An Autoformer is actually an *Auto-Transformer*. We just use the shortened version of the name when referring to them. Voltage Booster and Voltage Regulator are other commonly used terms for auto-transformer.

According to one of the first Autoformer manufacturers, "Autoformers are designed to increase the Voltage to your RV and help eliminate Low Voltage damage to your electrical appliances."

Another manufacturer stated, "Voltage Regulators automatically and continually monitor Line Voltage conditions and boost Voltage to an acceptable level, when needed, helping prevent Low Voltage damage to the RV's appliances and electronic devices."

While the "purpose" of an Autoformer is to protect your equipment from Low Voltage, there is a good deal of controversy about Autoformers. Whether or not an Autoformer "steals power," or if the Autoformer truly has a practical 10% to 16% boost capability, or even if such a small percentage of boost is worth the unit's price, I will not debate in this book. There are already plenty of online forums that will.

An Autoformer is only capable of boosting minor Low Voltages. More importantly, what I want you to know is that <u>none</u> of the Autoformers can automatically protect you from Wiring Faults!! (i.e., Open Ground, Reverse Polarity, Open Neutral, and Accidental 240V.) Yes, they may indicate to you, with simple diagnostic lights, if a Fault exists, but **<u>you</u>** must take decisive action to protect your electrical equipment and your RV (i.e., UNPLUG from the Post)!

An Autoformer typically provides limited surge suppression, only for itself – not for your RV. Their "RV" surge suppression feature only exists because the Autoformer uses a step-up transformer to do its job. A surge cannot be stepped up. It just "burns out" the transformer. And, by the way, Autoformers are very heavy. The 50 Amp models weigh between 40 and 46 pounds, and, in most cases, you must pay to ship the unit back to the manufacturer to have it repaired.

One last thing – All existing Autoformers do absolutely nothing to adjust (buck) the Voltage "down" if it is too high (> 132 Volts).

So, if you are thinking about getting an Autoformer, please read its operating/instruction manual very carefully, first. Call the Autoformer manufacturer if you have any questions or need clarifications.

ELECTRICAL PHASE

You may or may not have heard this phrase before. In the United States and Canada, electricity is generated in Three (3) Phases. Simplistically, it all has to do with positioning three coils of wire at equidistant positions on a stator (the stationary part of the generator) and a 2-pole permanent magnet on a rotor (the rotating part of a generator). Basically, "Phase" relates to the poles of the magnet rotating past the coils at different times as a function of electricity generation. And that is about as technical as we're going to get. We'll just consider the standard of "Three Phases of Electricity" as one of those "Laws of Physics" we cheerfully accept.

Electricity is also transmitted from the generator plant to the end-users in Three Phases. The next time you see a large electrical transmission tower, count the number of wires.

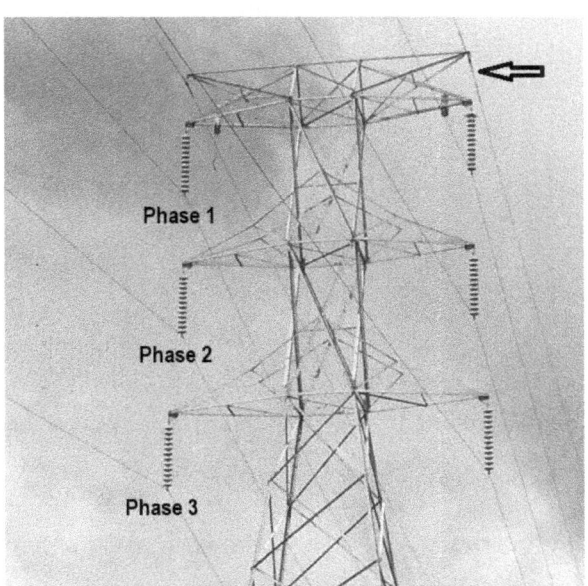

Two groups of Three Phase wires
(One group on each side)

Typically, you will see one or two groups of three (3) large wires (or possibly three groups of 2, 3, or 4 wires) suspended from the towers. (**Comment:** There will also be a smaller wire running above the three larger wires – this wire is the system's lightning rod.) Each of the large wires (or groups of wires) carries a separate phase of electricity. These phases are different (120° out of rotation) from each other, and because of this, the wires are physically separated. If they were to touch each other, there'd be a whole lot of arcing and sparking going on!

The vast majority of electricity end-users in the United States are domestic houses and small businesses attached to and operating on just <u>one</u> of the three phases (referred to as a "**Single Phase**") of the generated and transmitted electricity. Using all three phases to provide electricity to a large metropolitan electrical service grid allows more electricity to be distributed without being drawn down heavily. (**Remember:** Volts go "down" when Amps go "up!")

The 120-Volt electricity, used by the many apparatuses and most appliances in your home or RV, comes from an electrical state referred to as a "**Split-Phase.**" The electric company's step-down transformer kind of looks like a metal trash can (see above)

attached near the top of a power pole, close to the wires. It reduces the Voltage of a "Single Phase" Line "down" from about 7,000 Volts and splits it into two equal 120-Volt "Lines." Tying these "Lines" together (at your home, **not in your RV**) will provide 240 Volts (120V + 120V) for larger appliances (e.g., dryer, oven, & air conditioner). **Note:** Lines are not Phases, or, put another way – "Split-Phase" is not Two-Phase. Additionally, the two Output Lines from the step-down transformer are 180° **Out-of-Phase** to each other (when one is positive, the other is negative, and vice versa), not 120° apart like the generated Three Phase electricity.

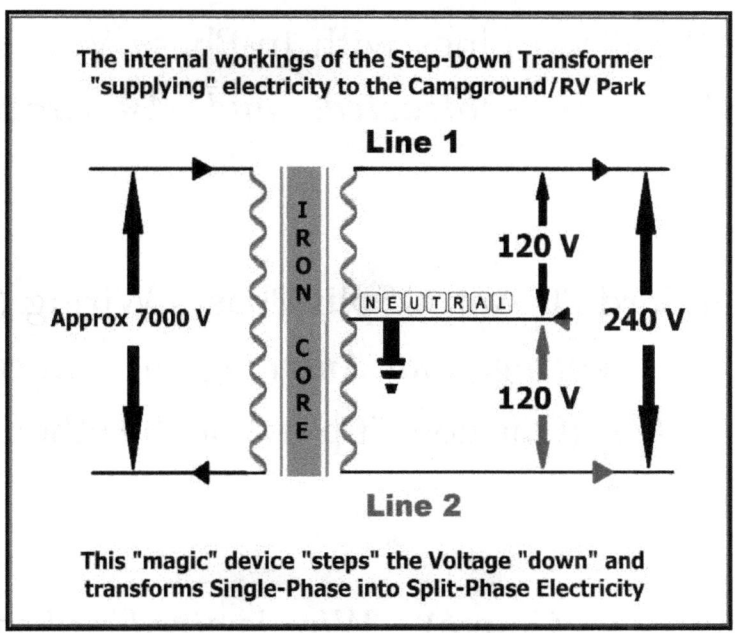

(**Comment:** So you know, Multi-Phase Electricity is non-existent in the domestic (house or small business) and RV environments. Multi-Phase electricity is typically used only in large, commercial environments where Voltages much higher than 240V are needed.)

Several electrical <u>Wiring</u> <u>Axioms</u> you should commit to memory:

1. Standard 50 Amp "Split-Phase" Wiring (Two Lines with Out-of-Phase Voltage) – *Voltage is added, and Amperage is subtracted.*

2. Adapting a 50 Amp RV "down" to a 30 Amp Outlet (Two Lines with In-Phase Voltage) – *Voltage is subtracted, and Amperage is added.*

3. Standard 30 Amp "Split-Phase" Wiring (One Line) – *Voltage and Amperage are inversely variable.* (One goes "up" while the other goes "down.")

4. Wire Size (Gauge) – *Wire is sized and safety rated for maximum Amperage, <u>not</u> maximum Voltage.* (A small wire can carry a lot of Voltage, but not a lot of current.)

How do you know if the Post's 50 Amp Outlet is really providing two Lines of Split-Phase electricity? Here is a simple test: Take a hand-held voltmeter and "probe" the Outlet's two "Hot" points. If the electricity is from an out-of-phase ("Split-Phase") source, you will measure something close to 240 Volts (added Voltage – L-1V plus L-2V). If it is from an "adapted" (see Axiom # 2, page 58) source, you will measure Zero (0) Volts (subtracted Voltage – L-1V minus L-2V). <u>GUARANTEED</u>!

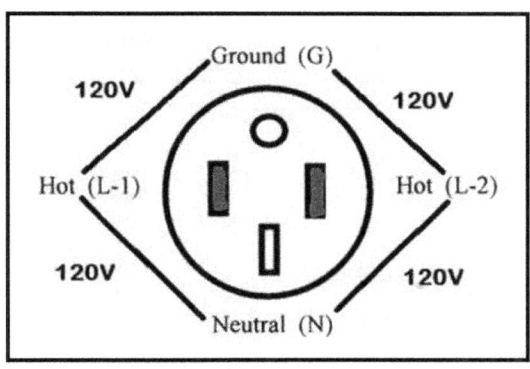

We, in fact, do want the two Lines of "Split-Phase" electricity at a 50 Amp Outlet. It is critical because of the size of the wiring. The 50 Amp Black, Red, and White wires are <u>all</u> 6 AWG (American Wire Gauge) in size. When we have two "Split-Phase" Lines for Out-Of-Phase Input Voltage and only one Line for the Output Voltage, the two Exiting Amperages are subtracted – the lower from the higher. The difference is the actual resultant Current Flow (e.g., if you are drawing 27 Amps on L-1 and 18 Amps on L-2, then the Neutral Line will only be carrying 9 Amps [27A – 18A = 9A].) And if both Lines are drawing equal loads, the result is Zero Amps on the Neutral Line. (e.g., L-1 Current Flow = 20 Amps, and L-2 Current Flow = 20 Amps, then Neutral Line Current Flow = 0 Amps.) "Ah-ha," you say, "that's why the output wire isn't larger than the two inputs. It won't have to carry more than 50 Amps! Right, you are.

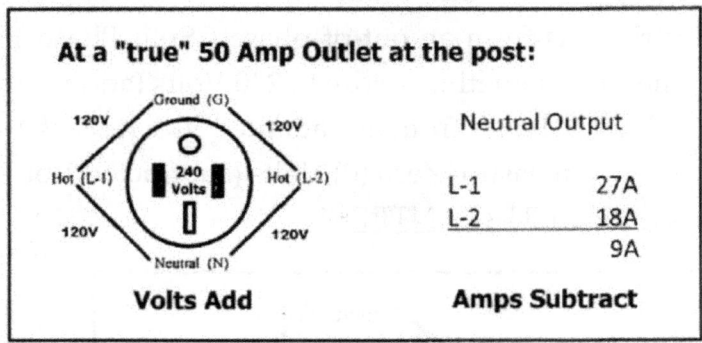

(Wiring Axiom # 1)

By the way, the 50 Amp Power Cord's Ground (green) wire **is** smaller than the others. It is only 8 AWG. That's because when a piece of equipment crashes internally (Shorts to Ground), there is no Current Flow, just errant electrical pressure (Voltage) escaping out the back door. (**Remember:** "The Ground Wire is **NOT** a normal path for electrical pressure [Voltage].")

Now, let's look at a significant problem that always occurs when we adapt a 50 Amp RV "down" to a 30 Amp Outlet. When we do so, we are plugging into just <u>one</u> of the Lines (referred to as an **In-Phase** Line) of the "Split-Phase" Voltage and trying to "mechanically split" it again inside the Adapter. Actual Phase-Splitting **only** occurs at the electric company's transformer – not at the Adapter. (**Remember:** The adapter provides equal electrical pressure down two Lines, just like the water wye.)

Besides the previously mentioned Zero Volts phenomenon, our adaptation also results in the Exiting Line Amperages being added together (L-1A + L-2A). And that is why it is so easy for a 50 Amp RV, when adapted "down," to "trip" the 30 Amp breaker at the Post. Or, if we exceed 30 Amps of Current Flow, and the breaker fails to "trip" correctly, the rubber surrounding the tines on our Adapter's Plug Head starts to melt from the heat of the excess Current Flow. Either way, we cause the excess Current Flow by running too much equipment when we are adapted "down!" *(Hmmm... maybe the burnt Neutral tine on your Adapter's 30 Amp Plug Head wasn't the RV park's fault after all.)*

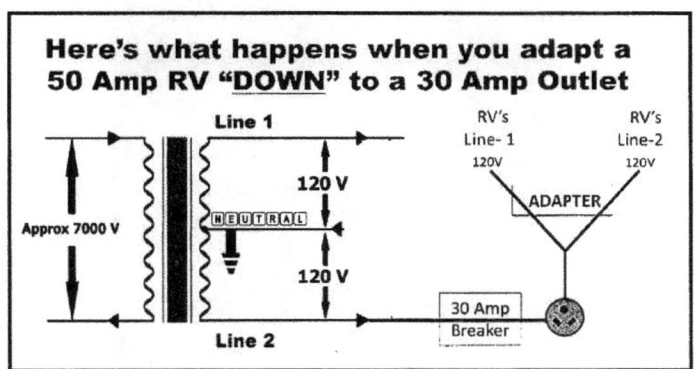

Sooo...

When you ADAPT a 50 Amp RV "down" (↓) to a 30 Amp Outlet, you **MUST** operate as though you are in a 30 Amp RV!

This is the reason WHY:

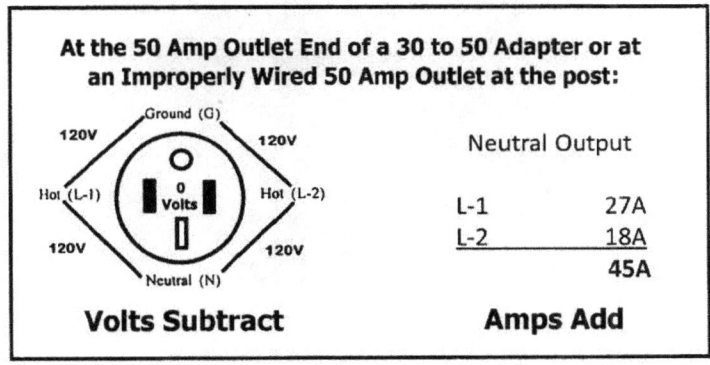

(Wiring Axiom # 2)

The resultant 45 Amp Draw exceeds the capability of the 30 Amp Outlet's Neutral Wire. Excessive Amp Draw results in high heat, and high heat can result in FIRE!

The excessive heat usually becomes visible as a severely burnt Neutral tine on the Plug Head and Neutral tine receptacle on the 30 Amp Outlet at the Post. Here's an unfortunate case study:

Burnt-out Neutral at the Plug Head

Burnt-out Neutral at the Outlet
(Images courtesy of Mr. Tim Enright [www.bugsmacker.com])

Most people typically blame the campground's Outlet rather than the genuine cause of this problem – a 50 Amp owner/operator, adapted "down" to a 30 Amp Outlet, and turned "ON" more electrical equipment than s/he should have. (**Comment:** The same kind of Plug Head/Outlet damage can also occur to a 30 Amp RV when its owner/operator unknowingly turns "ON" too much equipment.)

Here is the indisputable logic of "WHY" a 50 Amp RV owner should not do that:

```
  12,000 W  -  Maximum 50 Amp Electrical Capability
-  3,600 W  -  Maximum 30 Amp Electrical Capability
   8,400 W  -  A BIG Difference
```

- OR, looked at another way -

The difference equals a 70% Loss of Electrical Capability when adapted down.

Translation:

For safety's sake, you CAN NOT turn-on more than 3,600 Watts (or 30 Amps) of your electrical capability when your RV is adapted down to a 30 Amp outlet!!

Please, whichever Amperage your RV is wired for, don't be your own worst enemy! Everyone should pay attention to their total Amp Draw. When you fail to do so, you WILL have problems!

And just how are you supposed to do this? Well, let's go back to our Electrical Law of Physics:

$$\text{Power} = \text{Pressure} \times \text{Flow}$$
or
$$\textbf{Watts} = \textbf{Volts} \times \textbf{Amps}$$

Divide both sides of the equation by Volts.

$$\frac{\text{Watts}}{\text{Volts}} = \frac{\cancel{\text{Volts}} \times \text{Amps}}{\cancel{\text{Volts}}}$$

The Volts to the right of the equal sign (=) cancel out and leaves us with the equation:

$$\underline{\textbf{Watts}} = \textbf{Amps}$$
$$\textbf{Volts}$$

(**Note:** This is the most important equation every RVer should know!)

Find the Wattage value (from the "label" on the equipment/appliance or the owner's manual) for each piece of 120 VAC equipment in your RV (including everything the OEM built into it, and especially all the extra "stuff" you moved from the house (or bought at a store) into the RV – especially cooking appliances) and write down the Wattage.

Next, divide each Wattage value by 120 (the Voltage standard from the electric company). The mathematical result is the typical number of Amps a particular piece of equipment draws when turned "ON."

Do this for every piece of 120 VAC equipment in your RV and make a list containing each equipment's name and its calculated Amp Draw.

Now, keep track of everything you turn "ON" and sum the Amp Draws. (Subtract the Amperage when you turn "OFF" a piece of equipment.) You should always check the list's total before you turn "ON" another piece of equipment. (**Remember This:** The breaker above the Outlet you are plugged into at the Post is not attached to the returning Neutral Wire and does not automatically react to any over-currenting you cause.)

In due course, you will learn when you can or cannot safely turn "ON" a piece of electrical equipment – without referring to the list – and that's when you will have truly become a "seasoned" RVer.

Some of you 50 Amp RVers are probably wondering about the **Intellitec "Load Shedding System"** you may have (or will soon wish you did have) in your RV. This system can sense the "adapted Split-Phase" Voltage measurement of Zero Volts between the two incoming Lines (Hmm...must be "In-Phase"). When it does, it assumes you are plugged into a 30 Amp Outlet and activates itself to keep track of total Amp Draw (Intellitec's sensor encircles the outgoing Neutral Wire – looking for the "added together" Amperages). Now, it can start shedding loads to help prevent you from accidentally tripping the 30 Amp breaker at the Post. Be aware, though. It cannot tell the difference between 30 Amp and 20 Amp incoming Voltage. You must manually change the setting with a switch. And, yes, when it senses the correct "Split-Phase" (50 Amp) incoming sum of 240 Volts, the system doesn't seem to work at all. That's because it does not worry about Current Flow or shedding loads when you are plugged into a correctly wired 50 Amp Service Outlet.

However, if you are absolutely positive you are plugged directly into a 50 Amp Outlet and the Intellitec system tells you that you are plugged into a 30 Amp Outlet, <u>trust the Intellitec display panel</u>. It is telling you the 50 Amp Outlet you are plugged into is wired <u>incorrectly</u>. This means only one Line of "Split-Phase" electricity is being used to provide Voltage to both L-1 and L-2 (just like the "adapted" concept mentioned before), and the Voltage difference is Zero. You can verify this problem with a Voltmeter. If it is genuinely an Outlet Wiring Problem, it would be best to try another site on a different row in the park and see if it is also wired incorrectly. Please, be sure to tell the management office about the problem so it can be fixed. **WARNING:** The excess Amp Draw caused by this predicament can also burn up/off a Neutral Wire in your RV's electrical system anywhere from your Circuit Breaker Panel back to the Outlet you are plugged into (i.e., somewhere between the electrical source and your Circuit Breaker Panel).

Now, for several **Bothersome Conundrums** you've always wondered about and wanted answers to:

As one of my customers said, "Admittedly, I'm cheap and like to adapt 'down' to 30 Amps to save a few bucks when plugging in my 50 Amp RV. Just how does a 50 to 30 Adapter work?" (**Comment:** First of all, in reality, it is a **30 to 50 Adapter**. [Even the manufacturers of these things get it wrong.] Just as Circuit Breakers are always located at the source of electrical pressure for safety, the correct way to identify an Adapter is to start at the source – with the Plug Head. Since we will be plugging the Adapter into a 30 Amp Outlet [the source of electrical pressure], that's the number we should reference first.

Therefore, it is a 30 to 50 [30M to 50F] Adapter. **Note:** A 50 to 30 [50M to 30F] Adapter is used by a 30 Amp RV when adapting "up" to a 50 Amp Outlet.)

To answer how an Adapter works, I will first ask you to review the information about the "wye" splitter in our water example (see pages 3 & 8). {I'll wait here while you do.}   ...Okay, then, when you insert the 30 Amp Plug Head end of an Adapter into the Outlet, you will, obviously, be connecting to only one Hot Line of electrical pressure. This one Hot Line runs to the 50 Amp Outlet end of the Adapter. The electrical pressure is physically "wyed" to the two different Hot Lines necessary for 50 Amp Service – giving you equal electrical pressure (Voltage) down both Lines.

Some people, erroneously, want to insist they get 25 Amps on each Line. What you truly have are two Lines of 120-Volts of electrical pressure, with a maximum <u>total</u> Amp Draw capability of only 30 Amps – limited by the breaker at the Post. (And, **NO**, it is <u>NOT</u> 15 Amps capable on each Line [15 + 15 = 30], either.) **Remember:** Amp Draw depends on how much equipment is "turned-on" on each Line inside the 50 Amp RV. AND, it's cumulative when we adapt "down" – Line 1's Amp Draw <u>plus</u> Line 2's Amp Draw <u>cannot</u> be higher than the Outlet's breaker's 30 Amp set-point.

Next, he said, "Well, what about those Cheater Boxes? I can get 50 Amps out of one of them, can't I?"

A "**Cheater Box**" is a connection device with two 30 Amp Plug Heads attached to a box with a 50 Amp Outlet mounted in it. You could also put a 15M to 30F or 20M to 30F Adapter onto one or both 30 Amp Plug Heads.

"Cheater Box"

This customer wanted to assume, if he plugs one of the Cheater Box's Plug Heads into a 30 Amp Outlet and adapts the other Plug Head into a 20 Amp Outlet, he will get 50 Amps out of the box's Outlet, just like out of the 50 Amp Outlet at the Post. This kind of logic only got him the proverbial, NOOOO! "But," he continued, "It's a 50 Amp Outlet! 30 plus 20 equals 50, doesn't it?" While the arithmetic part of his statement is mathematically correct, his underlying electrical assumption is NOT!

Here's WHY – Inside the box, the "Hot" from one of the attached Plug Heads goes to just one of the "Hot" connections (e.g., L1) on the 50 Amp Outlet. The "Hot" from the other Plug Head, of course, goes to the other "Hot" connection (e.g., L2) on the 50 Amp Outlet.

At the Cheater Box's 50 Amp Outlet, however, the total Amp Draw will <u>NOT</u> be 50 Amps on each "Hot" wire (50/50), for 100 Amps total, but, instead, the Amp Draw is limited to the circuit breaker above the Post's Outlet which each Cheater Box Plug Head is inserted into. The most you might get is 30 Amps on each Line (30/30), for 60 Amps total – assuming both Plug Heads are connected to a 30 Amp Outlet. (Obviously 30/20, for 50 Amps total, if you're using a 20M to 30F Adapter on one of the 30 Amp Plug Heads to drop "down" to a 20 Amp Outlet on the Post. [See Appendix # 2 for critically important information.])

Indeed, suppose the Cheater Box is plugged into two (2) 30 Amp Outlets. In that case, this will allow you to run a little more equipment in your RV (60 Amps total), but you won't be able to run as much as you can when plugged into an authentic 50 Amp Outlet (100 Amps total) – (7,200 Watts vs. 12,000 Watts). And, if you have one of the Cheater Box's Plug Heads adapted "down" to a Lesser Amperage Outlet, then that Line of power in your RV will be limited to the 20 or 15 Amps breaker'd at that Outlet. (Maybe it <u>is</u> a good idea to know which equipment is attached to which line inside your RV.)

<u>WARNING</u>: *A Cheater Box will not function for long if the power to the 20 Amp Outlet is "jumped over" or "hotwired" from the 30 Amp Outlet at the Post. (<u>GUARANTEED</u>!) Each Outlet must be sourced and breaker'd separately.)*

Note: *A Cheater Box will <u>**NOT**</u> function <u>at all</u> if one (1) of the Plug Heads is connected to a Ground Faulted Outlet (GFCI) at the Post! (Another GUARANTEE!)*

The last conundrum has to do with **Extension Cords**. More than once, I have seen RVers using an extension cord to reach a remote source of electrical pressure (Outlet). Most are using correct electrical logic, but I often see some trying to do something with an extension cord that <u>will not</u> work.

Here are just two examples:

1. Plugging in any RV while using a small diameter extension cord, usually 16 or 14 AWG, to reach a distant 20 or 15 Amp Outlet and then trying to run an air conditioner in the RV. You <u>cannot</u> run any High Amp Draw equipment (e.g., air conditioner, microwave, washer-dryer, space heater, hairdryer, etc.) with a small diameter extension cord in the line. And, the longer the extension cord, the worse the problem is because of something called "Voltage/Line drop." A converter or inverter/charger turned "ON" is certainly okay, and maybe the refrigerator, too. Turn everything else "<u>OFF</u>." And don't forget about the electric element in the water heater!

2. A 50 Amp RV's Power Cord is stretched out fully and adapted "down" to a 30 Amp extension cord. The 30 Amp extension cord completes the run to the RV Post. It is adapted back "up" to a 50 Amp Plug Head, which is inserted into the 50 Amp Outlet. (**Comment:** "Because, that way, I can still get 50 Amp power to my RV," is the typical, but incredibly wrong, explanation I hear for this unusual configuration.)

In both cases above, the well-meaning RVer has only succeeded in making a giant fuse out of the attached, lower Amperage capable extension cord. Once s/he exceeds the Current Flow capability of the extension cord, it will melt/burn-out, and might even cause a fire. (**Remember:** High Current Flow = high heat. And, the smaller the wire, the less current it can carry!)

And, let's not forget about the **Ground Fault Circuit Interrupt** (GFCI) Outlet we mentioned earlier.

Outlets in an RV are wired in series – just like Christmas tree lights. Any Outlet within four feet of a water source (e.g., sink, shower, or toilet) must be on a GFCI circuit by RV code. Usually, only one (typically the **first** Outlet in a circuit originating at the Breaker Panel or inverter [both a.k.a. the source] is the "Master of the circuit" and has the "Test" and "Reset" buttons.) (**Comment:** It's a good idea to locate your Master GFCI Outlet, as well as find out what Outlets are downline from it in the circuit – p.s. you may have more than one Master GFCI Outlet in your RV.)

A GFCI Outlet monitors the amount of current flowing from Hot to Neutral. If there is any imbalance (Current Flow "out" is less than Current Flow "in"), it trips the whole circuit. The trip setting is typically five mA (.005A or five thousands of an Amp), and it can react as quickly as one-thirtieth (1/30th) of a second. A GFCI interrupts power fast enough to prevent a deadly amount of Amperage from passing through you. You may receive a painful Voltage shock, but you should not be electrocuted or receive a severe shock injury.

All GFCI Outlets should be tested once a month to ensure they are working correctly and will protect you from a fatal shock. To test a GFCI Outlet, first, plug a simple nightlight into one of its sockets. Make sure the light is on, and then press the

"Test" button on the GFCI. The GFCI's "Reset" button should "pop" out, and the light should go "OFF." If the "Reset" button

"pops" out, and the light does not go "OFF," the GFCI has been improperly wired. (Have a certified RV tech or a certified electrician correct the wiring error.) If the "Reset" button does not "pop" out when the "Test" button is pressed, the GFCI is defective and should be replaced. If the GFCI is functioning correctly, the lamp goes "OFF." Press the "Reset" button to restore power to the Outlet (as well as to the rest of the down-line circuit).

Contrary to popular belief, if a GFCI has unexpectedly "tripped," and it will not reset, the GFCI Outlet is probably not faulty and should not be blindly replaced. It usually will not reset because a piece of equipment plugged in somewhere in its circuit has a minor Short to Ground, and the GFCI is sensing it. Unplug the equipments connected to the circuit – one piece at a time, starting at the GFCI – and try to reset the GFCI after each piece is unplugged. Once the guilty piece of equipment has been removed, the GFCI will reset.

WARNING: The GFCI Outlet must be installed a specific way. If it is installed "backward," it will not work. (**Remember:** GFCIs do not like Reverse Polarity!)

Finally, we have come to the topic of **Electrical Protection** for RVs.

(**Comment:** I am sure you have heard or read about the horror stories of electrical damage happening to other RVers. Nevertheless, it still amazes me how many people think they "don't need any protection" from the, so far, unencountered electrical problems that **are** out there. Or even worse, "It won't happen to us!" And the most incredulous one I've ever heard, "It's already happened to us, so it won't happen again!" Whaaaat????)

In light of the majority of responses I get when I mention electrical protection, I say, again,

>"When it comes to damaging outside electricity, ignorance isn't bliss, my friends; it **is** expensive!"

120-Volt Electrical Protection

YES, it does "exist!" And **NO**, RV Manufacturers typically do not install it when the RV is built. (**Comment:** In fact, more than 90% of all RVs do not come with any type of electrical protection installed!) The manufacturers' reluctance stems from the perception that electrical protection has "No 'Wow' factor" for the female customers and no understanding of 'Need' by the male customers. Therefore, electrical protection doesn't sell RVs." As a result, third-party, after-market purchase and installation are your best bet for the appropriate electrical protection of your RV investment.

There are a number of manufacturers of products that most people commonly (although erroneously) call "surge protectors." I refer to the 'multitasking' protection devices as "Whole RV, **Electrical Protection Units (EPUs)**." They monitor for and stop the electrical problems trying to 'attack' your RV from the Post (obviously more than just surge suppression). Simple "surge protectors" do not automatically protect your RV from High/Low Voltages and Wiring Faults. (**Remember:** The probability of a Surge occurring has a much smaller percentage assessment than either High/Low Voltage problems or any of the four possible Wiring Faults.)

The two (2) leading manufacturers of "Whole RV, Electrical Protection Units (EPUs)" are:

Progressive Industries
(*progressiveindustries.net*)

and

Southwire Company
(*rvpower.southwire.com*)

Both companies have information about their units posted on their websites. Please, read and compare carefully. Only then can you decide which product/manufacturer you would prefer to have working to protect you and your RV. By all means, telephone either manufacturer if you have any unresolved questions or concerns after reading their literature.

(**Special Comment:** Both companies' Whole RV, Electrical Protection Units are <u>one-direction</u> sentries – they <u>only</u> guard against electrical problems coming **from** the Post. The EPUs are neither affected nor respond to any electrical issues "<u>inside</u>" the RV! [Please, reread this whole Special Comment. *<u>It contains an essential piece of information you must understand and always remember!</u>*])

Progressive Industries'
Electrical Management System™

Hardwire unit with Remote Display
(Model: EMS-HW50C)

Hardwire unit with Integrated Display
(Model: EMS-LCHW50)

(Images Courtesy of Mr. Tommy Fanelli)

New Portable unit with Integrated Display
& All-Weather Shield
(Model: EMS-PT50X)

(Image Courtesy of Mr. Tommy Fanelli)

All three (3) model types are available for 30 Amp and 50 Amp Services (just substitute 30 for 50 in the model number). Electrically and mechanically, the model types are the same. Still, they have different configurations to accommodate customer installation desires and/or needs.

Features of Progressive Industries' EMS™

Information Display Panel: Repeatedly scrolls updated readings of all applicable shore power information (Voltage, Amperage, Hertz, Error Code, and Previous Error Code). (**Comment:** Each model has a three-digit panel where the information is displayed, with a two-second delay at each data point, for easily understood readouts. If there is no Previous

Error Code to report, you will see a two-second "blank" space, instead.)

Time Delay for the A/C Compressor: Whenever the shore power is initially plugged into, interrupted by the source, or suspended by the EMS due to a Fault situation, a built-in time delay is triggered. A small blinking "dot" in the lower right corner of the display window indicates the time delay is in progress. (**Comment:** This time delay allows any head pressure to bleed off the Air Conditioner compressor before [re]starting.) The Portable Models are fixed with a 136-second delay (two minutes and sixteen seconds), but there are two possible settings for the time delay on each of the Hardwire Models; a user-selectable 136 seconds or the default 15 seconds from the factory. **Note:** The 15-second delay can only be used **IF** your RV's thermostat has a digital display window. The digital display thermostats have their own programmed compressor protection time delay.

Open Neutral Protection: If an Open Neutral condition is detected, *the display will not light up*; however, the EMS will instantly prevent this "bad" power situation from affecting the RV. (**Comment:** There is no error code for "Open Neutral" – you will just see a blank display screen. This could be misconstrued to be a "No Power" situation, but always assume the worst. "No Power" won't hurt your RV; however, an "Open Neutral" will!)

Reverse Polarity Protection: If the shore power is in a Reverse Polarity (miswired) state, the EMS will instantly prevent any "bad" power from entering the RV via the "exit" path, and the display panel will indicate the applicable error code.

Open Ground Protection: If the shore power is in an Open Ground state, the EMS will instantly prevent this "bad" situation from affecting the RV (and possibly you). The display panel will indicate the applicable error code.

High/Low Voltage Protection: When the shore power falls below 104 Volts for six (6) seconds or immediately rises above 132 Volts, the EMS will shut down power to the RV. The display panel will indicate the actual shore power Voltage and the applicable error code.

Accidental 240V Protection: If 240 Volts are detected on the shore power, the EMS will instantly prevent this "bad" situation from affecting the RV or "shut off" the shore power if already connected. The display will indicate how high the Voltage is and the applicable error code. (**Comment:** Once the incoming Voltage returns to a "within spec" level and stays there for the duration of the time delay, shore power will automatically be allowed back into the RV.)

<u>WARNING</u>: You should NEVER by-pass the EMS when 240 Volts is indicated! If you choose to do so, you will expose your RV and all of its electrical equipment to instantly damaging and extremely High Voltage.

AC Frequency Protection: If the shore power frequency (cycles) wanders (+ or − 9 Hz) from 60 cycles per second (60H on the screen), the EMS will instantly shut down the shore power and display an applicable error code on the display panel. (**Comment:** Hertz [Hz or H] is the unit of measurement for frequency. I have never seen anything but 60H in the United States and Canada; however, Mexico is another story!)

Previous Error Code: This feature informs the user why the EMS previously interrupted shore power to the RV. The Previous Error Code goes away when the shore power is disconnected from the RV. (**Comment:** If a different error code is generated before the RV is disconnected from shore power, the Previous Error Code will be over-written by the "new" Previous Error Code.)

By-pass Switch: Every **Hardwired** EMS model manufactured has its own by-pass capability. On the **HW** models, the switch is located on the remote information display panel. It allows the user to bypass the EMS's motherboard in the event of circuit failure, thus allowing source power into the RV. (**Comment:** The HW's remote information display panel reads "OFF" when the by-pass switch is activated. This does not mean the display is "OFF," but rather the motherboard's protective functions [Open Neutral, Open Ground, Reverse Polarity Accidental 240, and High/Low Voltage] are entirely "*OFF- LINE.*" [However, the protective Surge Suppression function is not disabled.] The **LCHW** model's optional by-pass switch does not change the display reading.)

Modular Design: Replacement parts are designed for simple plug-and-play installation, making "in-the-field" repairs (of the Hardwire units only) extremely user-friendly. (**Comment:** Because the Portable units are "weather-sealed," they must be sent to the factory for testing, repair, and resealing.)

Surge Suppression: All the 30 Amp and 50 Amp models have built-in Surge Suppression Modules. These modules are circuit boards with metal-oxide varistors (MOVs) and fuses attached. A MOV contains a ceramic mass of zinc oxide grains and other metal oxides, with one incoming and one outgoing wire attached. Each varistor is surface coated with epoxy. Their function is to protect against excessive Transient Voltages (spikes). The 30 Amp module is rated at 1,790 Joules (good for about 44,000 Amps of surge current), and the 50 Amp module is rated at 3,580 Joules (suitable for a whopping 88,000 Amps of surge current).

Surge Replacement Indicator: If a power surge ever damages the surge suppression circuit card within the EMS, the display panel will display an applicable error code indicating it needs to be replaced. (**Comment:** All Surge Suppression Modules ultimately die when they absorb more than their maximum capacity of High Transient Voltage [spikes].)

Warranty: All Progressive Industries' EMS models have a lifetime warranty. This is a non-transferable Lifetime Warranty. It applies only to the original owner and covers only those products purchased from an authorized dealer, retailer, or seller. This warranty covers manufacturer defects in materials and workmanship. Proof of purchase is now required for all warranty claims.

Progressive Industries'
Error & Caution Codes

E_0 → This represents the **Normal Operating Condition**. (**Comment:** Zero Errors. This is what you want to see!)

E_1 → Reverse Polarity Condition. Hot and Neutral Wires are reversed. (50 Amp - You must manually test to find out which one.)

E_2 → Open Ground. Ground Wire connection is nonexistent.

E_3 → Line 1 Voltage High. Voltage is above 132 VAC.

E_4 → Line 1 Voltage Low. Voltage below 104 VAC.

E_5 → * Line 2 Voltage High. Voltage is above 132 VAC.

E_6 → * Line 2 Voltage Low. Voltage is below 104 VAC.

(**Note:** Report the "meaning" of any of the above codes [**E_1** through **E_6**] to the Campground's Management. Progressive's Tech Support CAN NOT help with the above issues.)

E_7 → High Line Frequency. Frequency is above 69 Hertz (> 69Hz). (Hertz/Hz/H, a.k.a. cycles per second.)

E_8 → Low Line Frequency. Frequency is below 51 Hertz (< 51Hz).

E_9 → Data Link Down. The Remote Display (HW Models only) is not communicating with the EMS's motherboard. Call PI's Tech Support.

E10 → Replace the Surge Suppression Module. Definitely call PI's Tech Support.

(**Note:** Contact Progressive's Tech Support for help with any **E_7** through **E_10** Error Codes.)

* The "E_5" and "E_6" Error Codes are only applicable to the 50 Amp Models.

Have a Question?
Progressive Industries' Technical Support
Phone: 1-800-307-6702, press 2

If the EMS cuts the power to the RV, it will automatically restore power after the problem is resolved. Before the time delay is completed, a not previously seen data display, a "**P**" Code, will be evident immediately after the "normal" E_0 Code – e.g., **PE4**. This denotes the **P**revious Error Code or why the EMS shut down the power. (**Comment:** A total loss of power at the Post will <u>not</u> have a "**P**" code after the power comes back "ON.")

(**Comments** concerning both leading manufacturers' "Whole RV, Electrical Protection Units [EPUs]":

YES, if you own a 50 Amp RV, the 50 Amp EPUs are <u>fully functional</u> when adapted "down" to a 30 Amp power source at the Post. And, of course, if you own a 30 Amp RV, the 30 Amp EPUs are also <u>fully functional</u> when adapted "up" to a 50 Amp power source at the Post. [**Hint:** If you own a 30 Amp RV and expect to upgrade to a 50 Amp sometime in the future, save yourself the ultimate expense of buying one size of EPU, now, and then the other, later.]

<u>**WARNING**</u>: you <u>CANNOT</u> use a 30 Amp EPU to protect a 50 Amp RV! (That's 100% REALITY!) **Remember:** The extension cord conundrum #2 [on page 70].)

Southwire's "Standard"
Surge Guard Power Protection™

Important Note: The manufacturer (previously offering Surge Guard® products under the name of Technology Research Corporation [TRC]) did not, on one occasion (the transition from First Generation to Second Generation products), change their Model Numbers when they upgraded their electrical protection units. To counteract their oversight, please read the following few paragraphs to ascertain which Appendix of this book you may need to refer to for the operational functions of an older unit you may already have or inherited when you purchased a previously owned RV.

If you own a **Portable** Surge Guard RV Power Protection Unit with a Model Number of 34830 (30 Amp) or 34850 (50 Amp) and...if your **Portable** unit is very "rectangular," in shape, with the Plug Head and Outlet attached to protruding wires extending from opposite ends of the unit, and...

    1. If your **Portable** model does not have an LCD information display screen, see Appendix # 5 (First Generation). Or...

    2. If your **Portable** model has an LCD information display screen, see Appendix # 6 (Second Generation).

Suppose you own a Hardwire Surge Guard RV Power Protection Unit with a Model Number of 34520 (30 Amp) or 34560 (50 Amp). In that case, you will also need to know how many lights are on the front panel and which side they are positioned on (right only or both), and...

    1. If your **Hardwire** model has two (2) columns of lights (one column on each side), see Appendix # 5 (First Generation).

2. If your **Hardwire** model only has one (1) column of lights (right side only), see Appendix # 6 (Second Generation).

Southwire's "Current Generations" of "Standard"
Surge Guard RV Power Protection™

Note: Illustrative Labels of the "Current Generations" of 30 Amp and 50 Amp "Standard" Surge Guard RV Power Protection Units are displayed. The **Portable** units have "greenish" labels, and the **Hardwire** units have "orangish" labels.

Fifth Generation
(30 Amp) **Portable Models** (50 Amp)

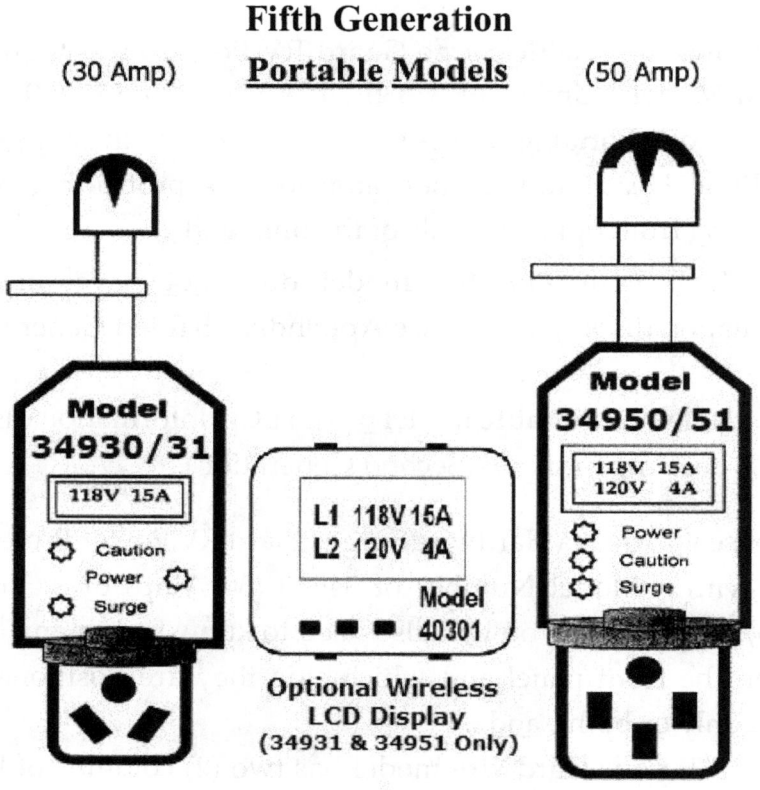

Southwire's Newest Innovation: The Wireless (Bluetooth®) LCD Display (Model 40301) is compatible only with the Portable Models 34931 and 34951. This display automatically detects the portable unit and provides pertinent information about everything the unit is monitoring. (Models 34931 and 34951 provide all the total electrical protection and features of the Models 34930 and 34950.) The display uses 3-AAA batteries, comes with an optional mounting bracket, and has a range of 100 feet. (**Comment:** Great for knowing what's going on at the Post in the middle of the night or during a stormy day.)

Fourth Generation
Hardwire Models

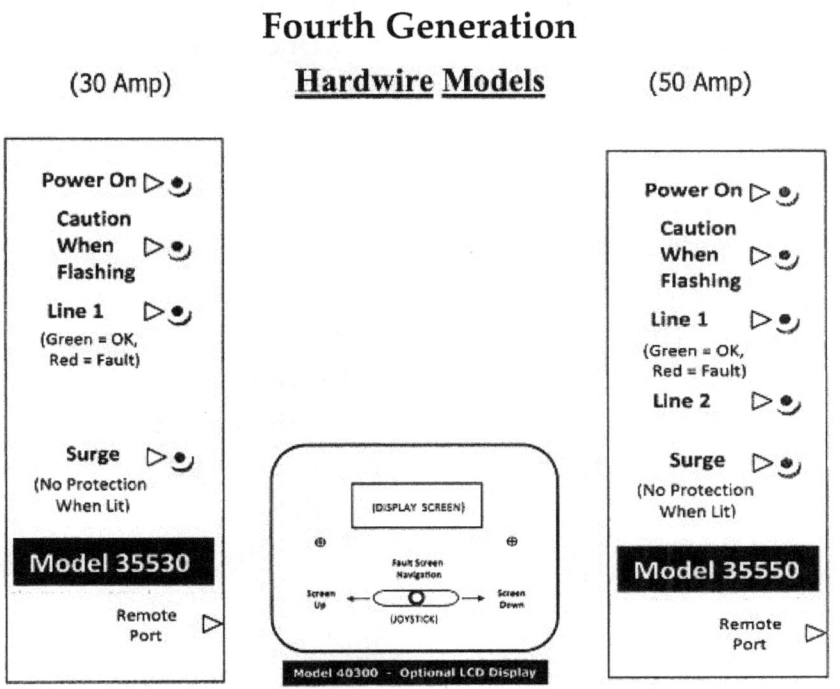

Important Note: The "Standard" Surge Guard **Hardwire** units cannot be installed flat on their backs! This means the unit's back (rear wall) cannot be oriented downward toward the ground (parallel to earth).

Features of Southwire's "Current Generations" of "Standard"
Surge Guard RV Power Protection™

While the **30 Amp Portable** model has three (3) LED lights - Two (2) on the left side of the front panel and one (1) on the right side, the **50 Amp Portable** has three (3) LED lights on the left side of the front panel. In addition, both the **30 Amp and 50 Amp Hardwire** Models have three (3) in-common LED lights on the right side of the front panel. Thus, from top to bottom, the lights are:

1. "**Power On**" LED Light – This power input indicator light will illuminate *green* when power from the Post is supplied to the RV. Surge Guard's "safe" Voltage range is between 132 Volts maximum and 102 Volts minimum. If the Line Voltage is "out of spec" for more than 8 seconds, the Unit's Over/Under Voltage Protection monitor will prevent power from passing through into the RV. (See Time Delay Indicator below.)

2. "**Caution When Flashing**" LED Light

   a. As a **Time Delay Indicator** – On the **Portable** Models, this light will blink *red* once per second for ten (10) seconds. On the **Hardwire** Models, this light will flash *red* once per second for 2 minutes and 8 seconds (128 seconds) to indicate a prescribed time delay is "in progress" (this allows the Air Conditioner compressor to bleed off any head pressure). **Note:** While the **Portable**'s LCD display will count down from 128 to 0, the **Hardwire**'s LCD will display will count up from 1 to 128. (**Comment:** Every time power is applied to the Unit, the time delay will activate. If the Line Voltage[s] is/are "in spec," the Unit will allow power into the RV after the time delay is completed, and the light will go "OFF.")

   b. As a **Fault Indicator** – (Applicable to the **Hardwire** units ONLY! – This light flashes *red* if the Unit has detected a

"Miswired Post" or a "Current to Ground" condition. (**Comment:** This WILL prevent power from passing through to a 50 Amp RV only.) The LCD screen will also display "Reverse Polarity."

3. "**Surge**" LED Light – If the *Red* Surge light is "ON," it means NO surge suppression is available. (**Comment:** The internal surge suppression module has given up its "life" to protect you and your equipment. The other protection functions of the Unit will still work; however, Southwire recommends the entire Unit be replaced.)

The **30 Amp Hardwire** Model has the same three lights listed above, plus one (1) additional LED light on the right side of the unit (4 total). "**Line 1**" – When *green*, the L-1 Voltage is between 132 Volts and 102 Volts. When *red*, the Voltage is above or below the specified range of Voltage, and power is shut "OFF" to protect your RV.

The **50 Amp Hardwire** Model has the same three lights listed previously, plus two (2) additional LED lights on the right side of the unit (5 total). "**Line 1**" and "**Line 2**" – Just like the 30 Amp Model, the Voltage is between 132 Volts and 102 Volts when green. When *red*, the Voltage is above or below the specified range of Voltage, and power is shut "OFF" to protect your RV.

Surge Suppression – All the 30 Amp and 50 Amp models have built-in Surge Suppression Modules. Their function is to protect against excessive transient Voltages (spikes). The 30 Amp Units are rated at 2,450 Joules, and the 50 Amp Units are rated at 3,850 Joules. This suppression capability protects the RV's 120-Volt electronic systems and appliances from harmful spikes without disrupting the RV's power supply.

The **Portable** models' built-in displays have the following readouts:

LCD Display Screens – There are two alternating screens on the Surge Guard Display. The main screen and the secondary screen display different information.

1. **Main Screen, "Power Up"** – The top line will display 'DELAY,' and the bottom line will display the time delay's count-up, in increasing seconds, until it reaches 128.

2. **Main Screen, "Normal Operation"** – The 50 Amp Model will display Voltages and Amp Draws for L-1 and L-2. However, the 30 Amp Model only displays Voltage and Amp Draw for L-1; because there is no L-2.

    a. **Top Line of Text** – Displays information about L-1 in the following format: "xxx**V** yy**A**," where xxx and yy are numeric values, and **V** stands for Volts available, while **A** stands for Amps of current being drawn.

    b. **Bottom Line of Text** – Will display the Voltage and Amp Draw for L-2 (50 Amp only) in the same format as the top line of text.

3. **Secondary Screen, "Normal Operation"** – Displays "RV STATUS ON" or "RV STATUS OFF" on the top line and the Voltage of L-1 on the bottom line (e.g., "L1 120V").

4. **Main Screen, "Fault"** – If the Voltage coming into the RV is less than 102 Volts on either L-1 or L-2, then the main screen will display: "L1 LOW" or "L2 LOW," instead of the Voltage and Amp Draw. If the Voltage coming into the RV exceeds 132 Volts, the main screen will display L1 HIGH" or "L2 HIGH" instead of the Voltage and Amp Draw.

5. **Reverse Polarity** – If the Polarity of the Voltage coming into the RV is reversed, then the Surge Guard Unit will display "REVERSE" on the top line and "POLARITY" on the bottom line until this condition is corrected. A "Current or Voltage on Ground" Condition will <u>also</u> be displayed as "REVERSE POLARITY."

The following are "NEW" Display Screens:

6. **High Neutral Current** – Amperage on the Neutral return is greater than 65A (> 130%) on the load side. Find another power source! (i.e., Disconnect and then: <u>a</u>. move to a different site or <u>b</u>. start your generator.)

7. **Current High** – Amperage on the Neutral return is greater than 62.5A (> 125%). Find another power source! (i.e., Disconnect and then: <u>a</u>. move to a different site or <u>b</u>. start your generator.)

8. **Over-Temperature** – The Portable's Plug Head temperature exceeds the recommended operation (> 200° F). Find another power source! (i.e., Disconnect and then: <u>a</u>. move to a different site or <u>b</u>. start your generator.)

9. **Open Ground** – Ground Wire is missing or miswired. Find another power source! (i.e., Disconnect and then: <u>a</u>. move to a different site or <u>b</u>. start your generator.)

10. **Replace Surge** – The Surge module has given up its "life" to protect you and your RV (it's now "dead"). Call Southwire's Technical support.

The **Hardwire** models with the <u>optional</u> display installed (*Display Model # 40300 & Cable # 40258*) automatically exhibit the same Main Screens as the Portable models ("Power Up" and "Normal Operation"). However, during a "Fault" condition, the remote display unit has the additional capability of displaying a combination of one or more of 11 established Fault Code Indicators (refer to the owner's manual for a complete list). Each applicable Fault Code will be displayed for a 3-second interval before the following pertinent Fault Code is displayed.

The <u>optional</u> display unit also has a manual "Screen Navigation." This navigation capability is accessed by using the joystick lever on the front of the display unit.

Pushing the joystick to the "Right" will scroll the "Main" screens (one screen at a time – push the joystick, again, to advance to the next screen) in the following order:

>L-1 Voltage
>L-2 Voltage
>L-1 Amp Draw
>L-2 Amp Draw
>View Faults

Pushing the joystick to the "Left" will scroll the "Main" screens in reverse order.

When the "View Faults" screen is displayed, pushing "Down" or "In" on the joystick will cause recorded (stored) Faults in the unit's memory to display (one Fault at a time – push the joystick to the "Right" to advance to the subsequent Fault or "Left" to reverse the order). The most recent Fault to have been recorded is labeled as Fault 1, the Fault recorded prior to this is labeled as Fault 2, and so on. The unit can store up to 16 Faults before it discards the oldest Fault (Fault 16) in order to add a "new" encountered Fault (Fault 1). Pushing the joystick "Down" or "In" again will return the display to the "View Faults" screen.

Need more help?

Southwire's Technical Assistance
Phone: 1-800-780-4324, Ext 20311

Recently introduced (2020) **by Southwire:** The Surge Guard RV **Automatic Transfer Switch Model 40430-RVC** with RV Power Protection. This model has been developed just for 30 Amp Service RVs. The functionality is the same as the 50 Amp ATS Model 40350-RVC; however, only for 120V, 30A, 60Hz service. (See coverage information on page 94.)

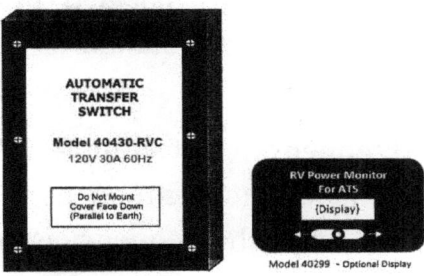

Three previously introduced "Enhanced" Surge Guard Units are illustrated below. (These units are only available for 50 Amp Service RVs.)

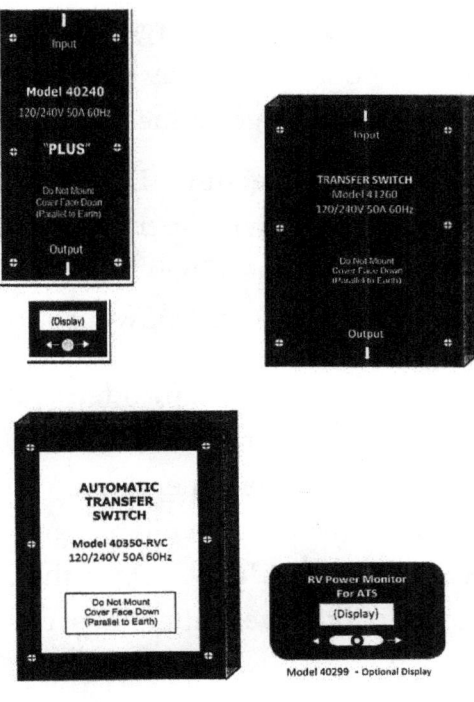

Important Note: The following "Enhanced" 50 Amp Surge Guard **Hardwire** units <u>cannot</u> be installed with the front panel facing down! This means the unit's cover <u>cannot</u> be oriented downward toward the ground (parallel to earth).

1. The **Model 40240** unit (originally labeled "**PLUS**") includes the following upgrades <u>above</u> the "Standard" units' capabilities (ergo the Plus designation)**:**

   a. **Over/Under Frequency Protection** – After a 30-second delay, the internal contactor (switch) opens to stop the flow of electricity into the RV when the frequency is outside a 54 Hz to 70 Hz range.

   b. **Remote Panel Indicator** – Easy to read 2-line, plain English, backlit LCD, remote display provides a visual indication of the Source Voltage, the load current (Amp Draw), or diagnostics.

   c. **Surge Suppression** – The surge suppression is rated at 3,350 Joules. The remote will display "Replace Surge" if a failed surge module or an open surge connection is detected.

   d. **Source Power Connection Diagnostics** – Contactor (switch) will not close (or will open if already connected to power source) if an Open Line, Open Neutral, Open Ground, or Reverse Polarity is detected on the power source.

2. The **Automatic Transfer Switch (Model: 41260)**, with **<u>Limited</u>** RV Power Protection, will transfer to either shore power or generator automatically when energized. In the event both shore and generator powers are available, generator power will dominate after a 30-second delay. Once the generator is shut down, shore power will activate after a 2-second delay.

(**Comment:** If your RV has a 50 Amp Hardwire, Model 41260, Automatic Transfer Switch installed, you do NOT have full electrical protection! Yes, the Model 41260 provides basic surge suppression of 2,600 joules [76,400 Amps]. However, the Model 41260 **only protects** from the following Wiring Faults: Open Neutral and Reverse Polarity. It **does not protect** from the other Faults: Open Ground, Accidental 240 Volts, Hi/Low Frequency, or Hi/Low Voltage. [**Recommendation:** If you, indeed, do have a Model 41260 Automatic Transfer Switch installed, your best protective course of action is to purchase either of the two manufacturers' **Portable** 50 Amp Electrical Protection Units and always use it when plugged into shore power.])

3. The **Automatic Transfer Switch** (**Model: 40350-RVC**), with Full RV Power Protection, is similar to the Model 41260; however, this unit provides all the following protections:

    Multi-mode Surge Suppression (fuse protected)
    Low (<102V) and High (>132V) Voltage
    Miswired Post
    Open Neutral
    Open Ground
    Reverse Polarity
    High and Low Frequency

The optional, 2-line plain English display *(Display Model 40299 & Cable # 40258)* uses LCD technology with a continuous visual indication of the Source Voltage (L-1, L-2), load current, or diagnostics.

Surge Guard Warranty – <u>All</u> Surge Guard units have a Limited Lifetime Product Warranty, covering manufacturer defects in materials and workmanship. (**Note:** The warranty extends only to the original purchaser and is non-transferable. However, if the unit was originally factory installed into the RV, it is transferable with the RV.) The Limited Warranty covers only products purchased from an authorized dealer, retailer, or seller. It does not cover used, salvaged, or refurbished products. All claims must include proof of purchase, including the date of purchase.

(**Comment:** If a Surge Guard Unit suffers a catastrophic failure and cannot allow power into the RV, the unit must be removed from the RV's electrical system. None of the Surge Guard models are field serviceable and, therefore, should be returned to the manufacturer for evaluation and repair. [**Remember:** Except for removing the **Portable** model from the electrical path, there is no longer a by-pass capability on any of the **Hardwire** Surge Guard Units.])

Personal Testimonial

My wife, Cindy, and I have been RVing for some time now (our FMCA number was issued back in 1981 – just five digits), and we full-timed for a decade (March 2002 through February 2012). And, yes, we did have electrical protection for our RV. It saved our "bacon" more times than we can recount. We encountered every possible Wiring and Voltage Fault that might be out there, some more than once. Here are just a few <u>unusual</u> examples:

1. At one campground in Virginia, we experienced a High Voltage Fault around 1:00 a.m. and a Low Voltage Fault around 5:00 a.m. – the same night. And we hadn't changed sites or Outlets at the Post!!

2. The Lowest Operating Voltage level we have ever found (after plugging-in) was 92 Volts – a busy campground in Maryland on a ridiculously hot Fourth of July weekend. We unplugged from the Post and, observing quiet hours, ran our generator instead.

3. An RV park in North Carolina was immensely proud that they had just upgraded their electric service to 50 Amps. When we plugged in, we had 123 Volts on Line 1, but only 9 Volts on Line 2. I guarantee you – nothing on Line 2 in our RV will run on just 9 Volts of alternating current! Adapting "down" to a 30 Amp Outlet resolved the problem for the night we were there.

(One Last **Comment** about either Manufacturer's Electrical Protection Units. We strongly advocate the following: A Whole RV, Electrical Protection Unit should **only** be by-passed when emergency situations warrant such an extreme measure and, also, **ONLY** when the manufacturer's tech support advises you to do so.)

(**Remember**: There is **NO** High/Low Voltage protection or Wiring Fault protection when any Whole RV, Electrical Protection Unit is by-passed or, physically, not in the circuit.)

STRONGEST WARNING: NEVER by-pass an Electrical Protection Unit when Accidental 240 Volts is indicated. Severe (and expensive) damage to the RV **will** result!

SPECIAL CAUTION: Please, do not confuse either manufacturer's Whole RV, Electrical Protection Units with **Intellitec's (PowerLine™) Smart Energy Management System**™. (You may already have Intellitec's system installed in your RV.) Intellitec's system is referred to as a "load shedding system." This system is only designed for one purpose – to help prevent you from "tripping" a 30 Amp Post breaker if you have a 30 Amp Service RV or when you are adapted "down" from a 50 Amp Service RV. The Intellitec system does **NOT** provide any other electrical protection!!

In response to the many questions I receive about the **Intellitec Smart Energy Management System** (a.k.a. Load Shedding System), the following simplification is provided:

This system is available for either 50 Amp Service or 30 Amp Service RVs. It is designed to prevent "tripping" the Circuit Breaker at the Post if the RV user inadvertently turns "ON" too much electrical equipment – meaning the total Amp Draw will be greater than the rated level of the Post's Circuit Breaker.

The Intellitec 50 Amp Smart EMS™ recognizes when electrical power is being supplied to the RV. Its diagnostic programming can determine if the incoming power is 50 Amp power, 30 Amp power, or Generator power. Suppose the incoming power originates from a 20 Amp source. In that case, the RV user must identify this lower power level by engaging the "30/20 Amp Select" switch on the display panel. The system **cannot** discern the difference between 30 Amp and 20 Amp power!

(The 30 Amp Smart EMS™ operates the same as the 50 Amp system but only deals with 30 Amp, Generator, or 20 Amp power.)

When functioning at 30 Amp (or lower) power, the system controls the "ON/OFF" operation for a maximum of four or six electrical loads (depending on the Model). These loads are characteristically "heavy" loads (i.e., High Wattage, therefore High Amp Draw). Their cumulative Amp Draw will trip the Post's breaker. Typical loads (in the order of lowest to highest priority) are the Electric Element in the Water Heater, the Rear Air Conditioner, possibly a Washer/Dryer, and the Front Air Conditioner. (Other appliances may be attached to the system in larger RVs. The Microwave, however, is traditionally not connected to this system or is controlled by the Inverter, if you have one.)

The system is also programmed to "memorize" the Amp Draw of each electrical load (appliance) attached to it. The system "memorizes" and stores the Amp Draw for each controlled load only when it is "**shed**" (turned "OFF" by the system). It subtracts the new total Amp Draw of the RV from the original total Amp Draw – the difference is the Amp Draw of the shed load.

The system continuously monitors the total Amp Draw. If it gets too high, the lowest priority appliance will be shed. If the Amp Draw continues to be too high (or goes higher), the next lowest priority load(s) will be shed until the total Amp Draw is below the Amperage limit of 30 or 20 Amps. This means no matter what order you turn appliances on, the Water Heater will always be shed first, then the Rear Air Conditioner, etc. The Front Air Conditioner is typically the last load to be shed. This is all done in the interest of protecting the RV from excessive Amp Draw.

When a load is shed, the appropriate "Power Status" light on the display panel may blink for the first two minutes. This blinking indicates a time delay to protect an air conditioner's compressor. Once the time delay is completed and there is enough power to operate the load, the light will turn "ON," and the appliance will be restarted. If there isn't enough power available, the light will turn "OFF," and the appliance will remain "OFF" until adequate power is available.

When plugged into a lower-level power supply (or running the Generator), the RV's total Amp Draw is displayed in a two-digit "Load Meter" window on the display panel. It behooves each RV user to check the existing Amp Draw before turning "ON" more equipment.

(**Comment:** The load shedding capability on a 50 Amp Smart EMS™ is <u>automatically deactivated</u> (turned "OFF") if 50 Amp power is being supplied to the RV. [**Remember:** Load shedding <u>only</u> occurs if a 50 Amp system is "adapted down" to a lower power source (30 Amp or 20 Amp) or operating on Generator power.] This means, when the RV is attached to a 50 Amp power source, the 50 Amp "Service Type" light on the display panel will be lit, as will all of the "Power Status" lights [all loads able to operate]; however, the "Load Meter" will be <u>blank</u>. Because the load shedding is deactivated, there is no need for the system to monitor the total Amp Draw and does not do so. So, my friends, when you are plugged into a 50 Amp power source, a "blank Load Meter" does not mean the system is broken, but, instead, is **working as designed**!)

Now, here's a bit of information you may not have considered before:

Lightning Surge entering via the "Jacks."

The National Weather Service states, "if you can hear thunder, you are susceptible to being hit by lightning – even if the sky is clear above you."

Because of the statement above, <u>*ANYTIME*</u> your RV's leveling or stabilizing jacks are "down," you should ensure a NON-CONDUCTING MATERIAL is between each jack pad and the ground. Why? Because your jacks are attached to your chassis – as are all of your electrical grounds – 120 VAC and 12 VDC!

When your jacks are "down," they make a positive connection to Mother Earth. When lightning strikes the ground, it can travel as far as 20 to 25 miles along a path of least resistance – and it does not know the difference between earth, an RV jack, or an electrical entrance/exit. Think about it – if lightning happens to find one of your jacks, your RV is fried!!

How does this come about? Well, as stated before, your jacks are attached to your chassis, just as all the electrical grounds are. Now you have a complete back door, electrical path for the High Voltage of lightning to follow from the earth to your equipment! The non-conducting material will interrupt the path and prevent the lightning from getting to your equipment via the jacks.

Central Florida, where we lived for over a decade, is known as the "Lightning Alley" of the U.S.A. Besides always using a Whole RV, Electrical Protection Unit, we are also fervent proponents of always putting a non-conducting material under your leveling (or stabilizing) jacks any time they are "down."

And that goes for the 5th wheel's "landing" gear and kingpin stabilizer legs, as well as the tongue jack on a travel trailer.

And it does not matter where you are in the country, what the weather is like when you "set up," or if you are parked on asphalt, concrete, gravel, grass, sand, seashells, wood chips, pine needles, or whatever. Our rule of thumb will always be: *"Jacks 'down,' non-conductor <u>always</u> beneath."* (*Comments:* **1**. Asphalt and concrete are man-made products composed of "earth" materials – a.k.a. conductors. And **2**. If you use wood blocks to help level up or stabilize a soggy/soft surface, the wood goes down first, and then the non-conductor goes between the wood and the jacks. [**CAUTION:** Wood, a naturally porous material, is a conductor when wet.])

One-inch (1") thick Jack Pads are staunchly recommended. However, the dimensional size depends on the Gross Vehicle Weight Rating of the RV – this helps distribute the weight and prevents cracking the concrete, pockmarking the asphalt, or boring the jacks into the ground.

1" x 12" x 12" pads for RVs < 16,000 lbs. GVWR.

1" x 14" x 14" pads for RVs ≥ 16,000 lbs. & < 26,000 lbs. GVWR.

1" x 16" x 16" pads for RVs ≥ 26,000 lbs. GVWR.

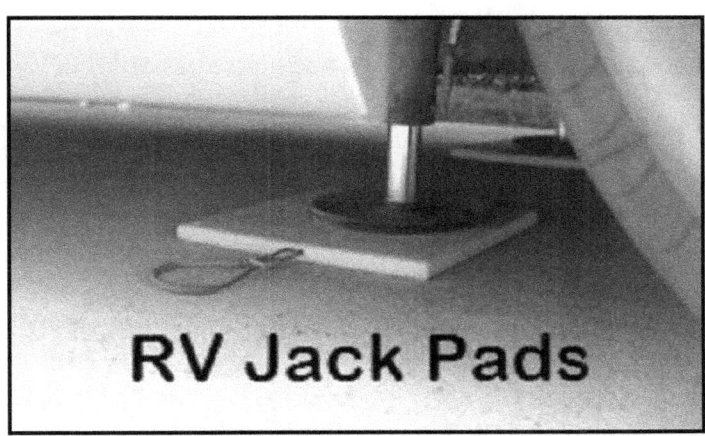

(Source: Outdoors for Life)
(annotated by Author)

The best, super-strong, industrial grade, plastic composite, non-conducting jack pads we've ever found can be researched at Outdoors for Life (*oflpads.com*). (**Comment:** Interestingly, for a few ducats more, you can have your name and phone number engraved into these RV pads – a great feature for the potentially "left-behind" pad[s]. [Oh, yes, I admit it; we left a set of jack pads behind at a campsite, two different times, during our decade of full-timing.] And, this company's pads are backed by an excellent warranty: "**IF IT BREAKS, THEY REPLACE IT – NO QUESTIONS.**"

UPDATE: A new and exciting jack pad is now available from RVSnapPad.com. Made out of finely graded, recycled tire rubber, their Snap Pads (appropriately named because they easily "snap" into place) attach permanently to a wide variety of RV leveling jacks, landing gear, and stabilizers.

Proudly manufactured in the USA, they offer ten different models and a multitude of sizes. They are available for round and square jack feet (all exteriors are octagon-shaped). They are sold as sets of 4; however, singles are also available. RVSnapPad provides a 2-year Limited Warranty with their product(s).

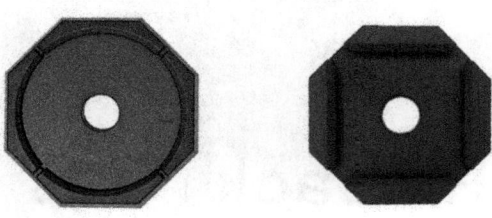

[Source: RVSnapPad.com]

A Quick Re-Cap of this *Primer's* Lessons

Electricity is easily understood when we use the model of:

Power = Pressure × Flow
(Watts)   (Volts)   (Amps)

When Amps go "up" (↑), Volts go "down" (↓), and vice versa, because the Wattage rating is a constant value.

It **is** important to pay attention to the "available" Voltage.

It **is also** important to pay attention to the total Amp Draw.

Circuit Breakers are safety devices that wear out with repeated use as "ON/OFF" switches.

High Current Flow (Amp Draw) results in damaging, excessive heat and possibly a devastating fire.

An RV wired for 50 Amp Service has two (2) separate incoming Lines of 120 VAC, each capable of handling 50 Amps. (That's 100 Amps TOTAL!)

The most dangerous thing you do while RVing:
"Plug into the Post!"

Post dangers include:

Open Ground
Open Neutral
Reverse Polarity
Accidental 240V
and
High or Low Voltage

An actual "Surge" affects everyone, not just one or two.

120-Volt Electrical Protection is very important.

*Here are a few impressive numbers
demanding your close attention.*

Maximum "SAFE" Wattage Limits:

A Typical 200 Amp Three-Bedroom Home – 48,000 Watts

A 30 Amp Service RV:

    Plugged into a 30 Amp Outlet – 3,600 Watts.

    Plugged into a 50 Amp Outlet – *Still* 3,600 Watts. *

    Plugged into a 20 Amp Outlet – 2,400 Watts.

A 50 Amp Service RV:

    Plugged into a 50 Amp Outlet – 12,000 Watts.

    Plugged into a 30 Amp Outlet – 3,600 Watts. *

    Plugged into a 20 Amp Outlet – 2,400 Watts.

    Plugged into a "Cheater Box"
    (depending on the Amperage capability of each Outlet plugged into)

        (30/30) – 7,200 Watts.

        (30/20) – 6,000 Watts.

        (20/20) – 4,800 Watts.

        (15/15) – 3,600 Watts.

Most Common Generators:

    5.5 kW – 5,500 Watts.   [*(OOPS!* Looks like most 50 Amp
    7.0 kW – 7,000 Watts.   RVs <u>cannot</u> run all their 120-Volt
    7.5 kW – 7,500 Watts.   equipment at the same time when
    8.0 kW – 8,500 Watts.   the generator is providing power!)]

*_FUNDAMENTAL FACT_:** If your RV is wired for 50 Amp Service, and you adapt "down" to 30 Amps maximum at the RV Post, you are downgrading/reducing your electrical capability by 70%! (**Comment:** Why would you want to restrict yourself this way during a long-term stay at a campground or RV park?? It bewilders me when I see so many people deliberately doing just that when 50 Amp Service is available at their site. [And they honestly wonder why electrical "things" in the RV do not seem to function the way they expect them to.])

(**Another Comment:** Maybe it is a good idea to find out precisely what the Wattage rating is for each piece of 120 VAC equipment or appliance in your RV. And don't forget about those "extras" you may have added to the RV. You know: the coffee pot, the electric skillet, the toaster, the blender, the popcorn popper, the electric coffee grinder, the heating cubes/space heaters, the air compressor, the electric drill, the deluxe hairdryer, the hair curler, the iron, the washer/dryer, the vacuum, and let's not forget about all those little "chargers" left plugged-in when it's not attached to the items they're supposed to be charging. The list goes on and seems to be endless. [**Remember:** Watts ÷ Volts = Amps.])

Wow! Imagine how many "amp hogs" most of us use in our RVs without realizing what we're doing to the available Voltage level at the Outlet where our RV is plugged in.

Unmistakably, electrical awareness is everyone's responsibility!! Protect yourself, your loved ones, and your RV by educating all RVing companions about indiscriminately turning "ON" electrical equipment in the power-limited RV environment.

Final Remarks: I fervently hope you have come to appreciate the impact of three crucial statements made earlier in this *Primer*:

1. "You <u>must</u> approach electricity 'logically' when it applies to RVs,"

2. "Pay attention to what you are doing," and

3. "When it comes to RVs and damaging outside electricity, ignorance isn't bliss, my friends – it's EXPENSIVE!"

Well, with those sobering thoughts, I will say we have finished your primer on 120-Volt RV "Shore Power." Hopefully, this book has encouraged you to seek answers to more complex electrical questions. That is great!! And, more so, this book has caused you to view RV electricity from a different direction. That's FANTASTIC!!

Since you now have a good handle on the basics, you are, indeed, ready to move on to a more advanced state of knowledge about your RV's 120 VAC electrical system. At this point, it is time to do the unthinkable. Yep, you guessed it – it is time to read your entire collection of equipment manufacturer's operating manuals/instructions. Enjoy!

Thank you for reading this *Primer*.

**May you always be
Wattage Wise,
Amperage Attentive,
Voltage Vigilant,
and an
Electricity Efficient
RVer.**

Sincerely,

Dale

A Veteran Owned and Operated Company
"Non Sibi Sed Patriae"

I sincerely hope you enjoyed this book. If you did, please comment about it on social media and, surely, write an Amazon or Goodreads review.

And, of course, please tell a friend about this book – especially if your friend owns an RV or is thinking about getting one.

Thank you for your support,

Dale Lee Sumner

p.s. You may want to check out the **RV Blog** page on my website: **sumdalus.com**

INDEX

TOPICS

Topic	Page(s)
30M to 50F Adapter –"How it Works"	66
About the Author	136
Appendix # 1 – For Safety's Sake! A Check List for examining the Campground's Post	112
Appendix # 2 – There is a difference between 15 Amp and 20 Amp Plug Heads and Outlets	113
Appendix # 3 – Labeling the MCBP's Hot Lines and Outlets in your RV	116
Appendix # 4 – WARNING about connecting Ground and Neutral to the same busbar	118
Appendix # 5 – First Generation of "Standard" Surge Guard RV Power Protection Units	122
Appendix # 6 – Second Generation of "Standard" Surge Guard RV Power Protection Units	127
Appendix # 7 – Third Generation of "Standard" Surge Guard RV Power Protection Units	134
Amps (Amperage) Definition	v & 10
Autoformer (a.k.a. Voltage Booster/Regulator)	53
Cheater Box	68
Circuit Breakers	21
Converter	51
Definitions & Terminologies	v & 9
Electrical Protection	73
Extension Cords	69 & 70
Ground Fault Circuit Interrupt (GFCI)	71

	Page(s)
Important WARNINGS	50
Intellitec's Smart Energy Management System	65 & 96
Inverter	51
Lightning Surge via the Jacks	100
Maximum/Minimum Voltages	13 & 15
Outlet Testing (30 Amp)	28
Outlet Testing (50 Amp)	36
Progressive Industries' EMS w/Smart Surge	75
Phase	55
Surge	46
Southwire's (TRC's) Surge Guard	83
Volts (Voltage) Definition	v & 10
Watts (Wattage) Definition	v & 10
Wiring Axioms	58
Wiring Faults, 30 Amp Service	25
Wiring Faults, 50 Amp Service	30

DIAGRAMS

30 Amp Electrical Service	27
50 Amp Electrical Service (with Converter)	33
50 Amp Electrical Service (with Inverter)	35
50 Amp Neutral Busbar	41 - 43
Power Distribution Panel	39
WARNING about the Sub-Panel Situation	120

APPENDIX # 1

(December 16, 2010)

For Safety's Sake

For the safety of your RV's electrical system and components, as well as your own personal safety, <u>before</u> you make a connection to any Outlet at any RV Campground/RV Resort/RV Park, etc., always make sure you . . .

1. Check to see if the Post's metal box is completely intact – no missing covers, no gaps or openings in the metal, and no rust through.

2. Check to see if each Outlet at the power Post has an associated Circuit Breaker. (There should be an exclusive breaker for each Outlet.) Turn "OFF" all of the breakers.

3. Check to see if each Outlet/Receptacle is physically unbroken – no cracks or missing pieces/chunks.

4. Check to see if there are any signs or indications of "burnt" or "scorch" marks on the front panel, anywhere around the Outlet(s).

NOTE: If you don't like what you see, DON'T plug in! Your safety, the safety of your family/guests, and the safety of your RV are in <u>YOUR hands</u>!!

Instead, report any discrepancies to the management office. Do NOT attempt to repair anything "on or in" the box, yourself. (**Comment:** And, keep your fingers and tools <u>out</u> of the box – remember, it does not belong to you!) **WARNING**: Intentionally interfering with or modifying any campground's RV Post functions without permission is considered to be Felony Trespass in many states.

APPENDIX # 2

(June 5, 2012)

There is a difference: Physically!

15 Amp Outlet & Plug Head

This Outlet's Neutral slot is the taller one on the left **and** the applicable tine on the Plug is also taller.

Vs.

20 Amp Plug Head & "Combination" 15/20 Amp Outlet

Notice, the Neutral tine on this Plug Head is rotated 90° **and** the Outlet's applicable slot looks like a "**T**" on its side.

And a difference: Electrically!!

15 Amps = <u>1800</u> Watts maximum

Vs.

20 Amps = <u>2400</u> Watts maximum

Caution: The "combination" 15/20 Amp Outlet, at the post, with its sideways "**T**" Neutral slot, implies you can plug in a 15 Amp Plug Head <u>or</u> a 20 Amp Plug Head into it.

<u>**SIGNIFICANT WARNING:**</u> <u>Always</u> use a 20M to 30F Adapter when plugging into a GFCI "combination" 15/20 Amp Outlet at the Post. Although the "typical" 15M to 30F or 15M to 50F Adapters will "fit" into a 20 Amp Outlet, they are <u>only</u> safety "rated" for a maximum of **<u>15</u>** Amps! If you adapt "down" with a 15 Amp Adapter, please realize the air conditioners, heat pumps, microwaves, convection ovens, and hair dryers (just to name a few High Wattage items) can draw much more than 16+ Amps when starting and/or running. Consistently drawing too much Amperage through a 15M to 30F or 15M to 50F Adapter will stress the Adapter to its burn-out or melting point. (**Remember:** The breaker above the Outlet is a 20 Amp breaker, <u>**NOT**</u> a 15 Amp breaker – the probability of a fire is extremely high!)

Despite this, the manufacturers of the 15M to 30F and 15M to 50F Adapters assert they may be used for **short-term**, "**temporary**" connections. To do so, absolutely and unequivocally, means **NO** usage of High Wattage appliances or equipment – the RV refrigerator and converter (or the inverter's charger) are okay, but that is about all! Therefore, the recommended and prudently safe practice is to use a 20M to 30F Adapter when adapting any RV "down" to a 20 Amp Outlet at the Post. There are two types:

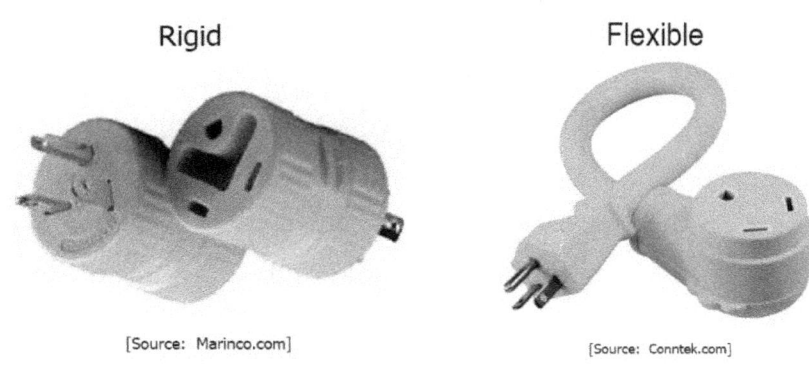

Rigid   Flexible

[Source: Marinco.com]   [Source: Conntek.com]

(**Comment:** I have never come across a 20M to 50F Adapter, and I am not sure they exist commercially. So, instead of adapting a 50 Amp RV "down" to a 20 Amp Outlet with a 15M to 50F Adapter, I strongly recommend you use a readily available 30M to 50F Adapter between your 50 Amp Power Cord and either type of the 20M to 30F Adapter [shown above] which you plug into the 20 Amp Outlet. The extra five [5] Amp capability (or the additional 600 Watts) gives you a considerable margin of safety, more ways than one!)

APPENDIX # 3

(February 14, 2016)

"I have a 50 Amp RV. How do I know which Hot Line is on which side of the Master Circuit Breaker Panel?"

It's up to you! That's right. It is your RV. You make the decision. Most Master Circuit Breaker Panels (MCBPs) are not labeled which side is which by the RV manufacturer.

When you first look at the MCBP, you'll see some sort of a distinct separation of the Circuit Breakers: Possibly, the Master Breaker at the top, near the center, and two parallel columns of breakers – one on the right side and one on the left side. Or, the breakers are lined up as one row – with the Master Breaker in the middle, placing half of the breakers to its right and half to the left.

I recommend you use the <u>front</u> air conditioner as the decision-assisting appliance. With 120-Volts supplied to the RV (shore power or generator power), turn "ON" the front air conditioner. Once it is running, go to the MCBP and turn "OFF" one of the 20 Amp breakers labeled as "A/C" (the typical annotation for the air conditioner). If the air conditioner stops, designate its distinct section of breakers as Line 1, and if the front A/C did not stop, designate the section of breakers as Line 2. (**Comment:** I use large, white Avery Dots to write "1" or "2" on and then stick them appropriately on the cover plate near the applicable line up of breakers.) You can double-check your decision by turning the first A/C breaker back "ON," and then, after the A/C is running, turn "OFF" the other 20 Amp breaker labeled A/C.

And, **"How do I know which Outlets are on which Hot Line?"**

With 120-Volts supplied to the RV, plug a simple (LED or Incandescent) night-light into the forward-most (closest to the front of the RV) Outlet and turn the light "ON" if it is not automatically lit. Go to the MCBP and locate the 15 Amp breakers labeled "RECP" or "GEN" (the typical annotation for Receptacle or General Use). There are usually just two (one on each Hot Line), but there may be more. If the light went "OFF" when you tripped one of the 15 Amp breakers, place an Avery Dot on the <u>Outlet</u> and label it with the number of the Hot Line (1 or 2) the breaker is located on. Repeat the same steps for all the other Outlets inside and any in the basement compartments. Then, you'll know which Outlets are fed by which incoming Hot Line.

(**Comment:** This simple system will also help you to know which Hot Line all of your "added" (i.e., not installed by the RV manufacturer) electrical equipment is plugged into.)

APPENDIX # 4

(July 4, 2017)

WARNING: When you plug your Power Cord into <u>any</u> Outlet, be it at your home, at a campground's Post, or anywhere else, the RV's Master Distribution Panel immediately becomes a Sub-Panel to the House/Campground/Other System!

This categorically means you CANNOT connect Ground and Neutral Wires to the same busbar (or run a wire from one busbar to the other) inside an RV. Why? Because <u>if</u> an Open Ground condition exists at the Outlet you plugged into, there is no direct Grounding connection to earth (only to the RV's chassis). Consequently, combining Neutral and Ground Wires in an RV <u>WILL</u> result in a dangerous "hot skin" condition, as well as possible electrocution!

Confused? I recommend you re-read the Introduction and about Open Ground in the "Possible Wiring Faults for 30 Amp RVs" section of this *Primer*, first, then continue reading this appendix's information.

Yes, houses and RVs are "two different worlds!" Here is another significant difference – a Grounding Rod.

(Source: patriotglobal.com)
(modified by Author)

A house has one because it is a stationary structure. (**Comment:** If you're not sure where your Grounding Rod is located, walk around the outside of your home, and you'll most likely find [probably somewhere near the outside wall closest to your home's Circuit Breaker Panel] the top of a steel rod sticking up from the ground with a clamp and a thick copper wire attached to it. And, if you look inside your home's Circuit Breaker Panel, you will find the other end of that thick wire attached to the Ground Busbar.)

An RV does not have a Grounding Rod because it is a mobile structure. (You know this because every time you stop for the night [or set-up camp], you never have to pound an 8-foot long steel rod into the ground. Then attach a thick connecting copper wire between the rod and the chassis of your RV before you plug your Power Cord into any electrical Outlet. [Rather bothersome, wouldn't you say, but think about attempting to remove the rod from the ground when you're ready to leave!])

Since it does not have its own Grounding Rod (a.k.a. "emergency back door/exit" for Errant Voltage), your RV must rely on the House/Campground/Other System you plugged into to provide one. Thus, we explain why the RV's Master Panel is now a Sub-Panel to the House/Campground/Other System.

A graphic depiction of how it is a Sub-Panel is on the next page.

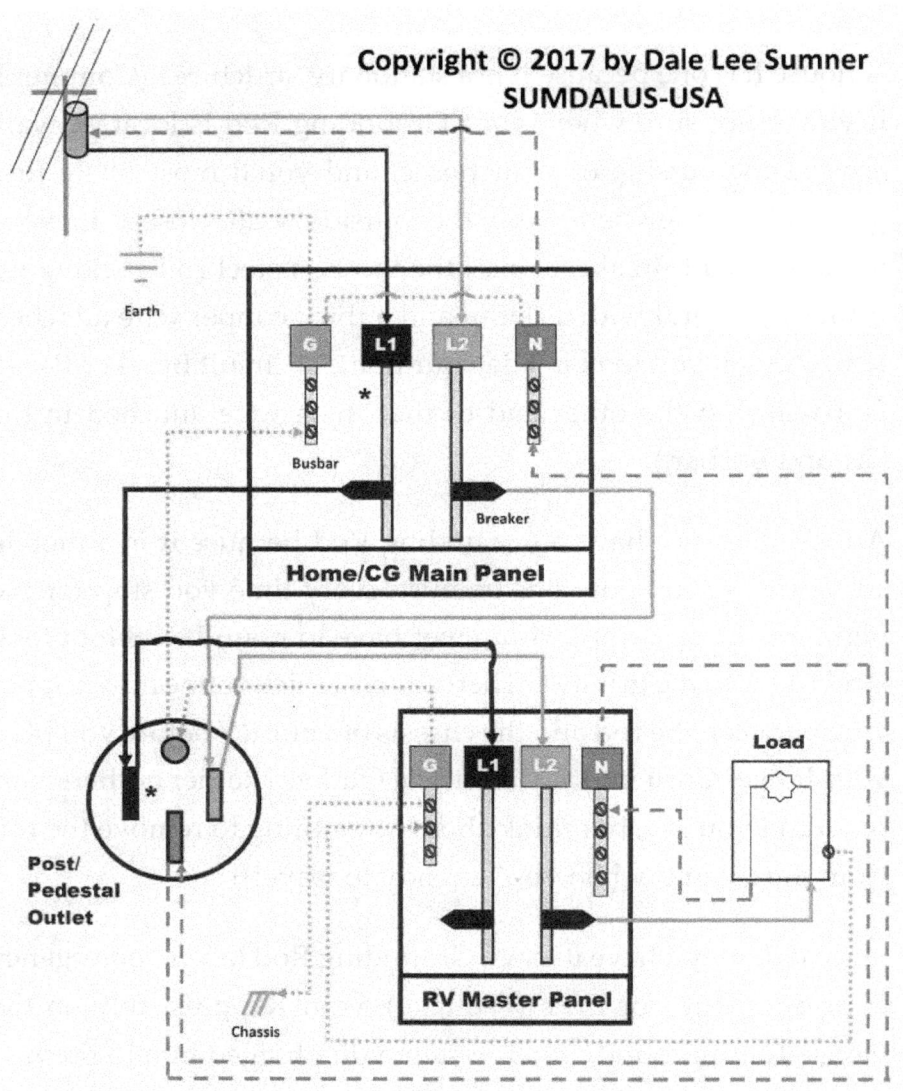

* Ignore L1 Connection for a 30 Amp System

Note: A color version of the above image is downloadable from the RV Blog page on my website: **sumdalus.com**

An Open Ground Fault at the "plugged into" Outlet prevents Errant Voltage (typically from shorted equipment in the RV or from transient spikes originating somewhere in the grid) from using the Grounding system to safely exit the RV.

Since knowing <u>before</u> plugging in is always safer, I strongly suggest using the Initial Testing procedures presented in this *Primer* to ascertain if an Open Ground exists at the Outlet you plan on plugging your RV into.

For a 15/20 Amp Outlet, you can use a commercially available 3-light "Outlet Tester."

After it's plugged into a 15/20 Amp Outlet, a tester will typically identify an Open Ground by illuminating <u>only</u> one of its three lights. Ensure which light is applicable by carefully checking the "code" panel affixed to the unit you use – not all Outlet testers are the same. (**Reminder:** YOU <u>**CANNOT**</u> USE THIS TOOL TO TEST FOR REVERSE POLARITY ON A 50 AMP OUTLET!)

Of course, the previously discussed Whole RV, Electrical Protection Units, will automatically make all the applicable Outlet checks at the Post and will not allow a house or campground Wiring Fault to cause costly damage to your RV's 120-Volt wiring and equipment.

APPENDIX # 5

(July 6, 2014)

TRC's "First Generation" of "Standard"
<u>Surge Guard RV Power Protection</u>™

The "First Generation" models of "Standard" Surge Guard RV Power Protection units are illustrated below.

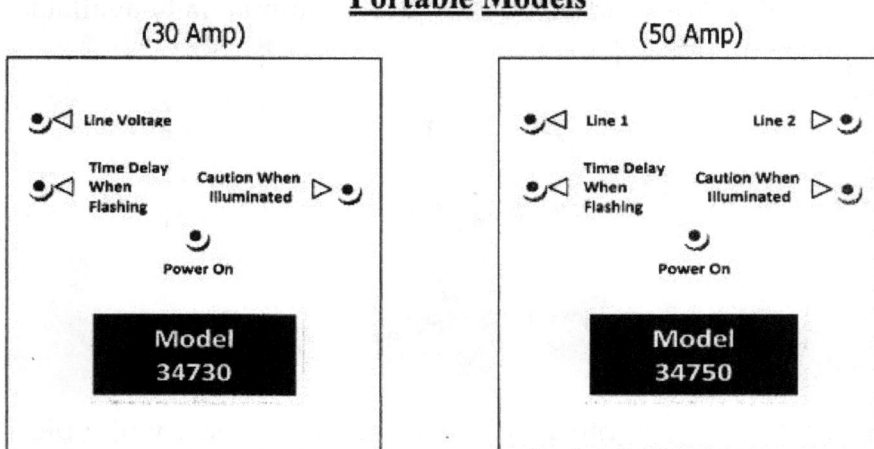

Portable Models
(30 Amp)   (50 Amp)

Model 34730   Model 34750

The **30 Amp Portable** is Lime-Green in color, and the **50 Amp Portable** is Blue-Green in color.

Note: There are <u>no</u> integral LCD Displays on these **Portable** units.

Hardwire Models

(30 Amp)   (50 Amp)

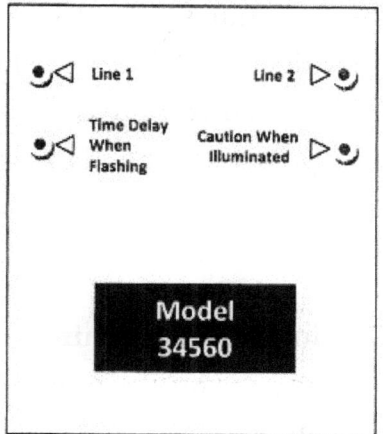

Note: There are no Optional LCD Displays for these **Hardwire** units.

The **30 Amp Hardwire** is Light-Orange in color, and the **50 Amp Hardwire** is Dark-Orange in color.

The **50 Amp Hardwire** had four (4) lights that provided information to the user. The **50 Amp Portable** had five (5). The **30 Amp Hardwire** had three (3), and the **30 Amp Portable** had four (4).

Both **Portable** Surge Guard Units have an additional light (located in the lower middle) to indicate some level of **Power** is available at the supplying electrical source.

Line 1 (and **Line 2** on 50 Amp units) – The light(s) illuminate when the Source Voltage on the indicated Line is within a specified range of 132 Volts maximum and 102 Volts minimum. If the Line Voltage is "out of spec," the light(s) will not illuminate, and power is not allowed into the RV.

Time Delay When Flashing – These light blinks once per second for 2 minutes and 16 seconds (136 seconds) to indicate a prescribed time delay is "in progress" (this allows the Air Conditioner compressor to bleed off any head pressure). Every time power is applied to the unit, the time delay would activate. If the Line light(s) is/are illuminated, the unit will allow power into the RV after the time delay is completed.

Caution When Illuminated – This light illuminates if the unit detects a Miswired Post, Reverse Polarity, or Elevated Ground Voltage.

(**Comment:** The Surge Guard literature states the unit will automatically shut "OFF" power for High/Low Voltage or an Open Neutral condition. However, when the Caution light is illuminated, TRC's troubleshooting guide states a Reverse Polarity or Voltage on Ground condition is present at the source power. [The unit will only stop power from entering an RV through a 50 Amp Surge Guard unit.] The recommended solution for both the 30 Amp and 50 Amp Models is to find another power source! [i.e., Disconnect and then: **a.** move to a different site or **b.** start your generator.])

Surge Suppression – Each "Standard" model is capable of excess energy (surge) suppression. The 50 Amp Model is rated at 1,750 Joules, and the 30 Amp Model is rated at 1,050 Joules.

Surge Guard Warranty – All models of the First Generation of Surge Guard RV Protection units had a Limited Product Warranty for one (1) year.

(**Comment:** If a Surge Guard unit fails, the unit must be removed from the RV's electrical system. None of the Surge Guard models are field serviceable and must be returned to the manufacturer for evaluation and repair.)

Critical Note: An especially crucial mounting requirement for "Standard" Surge Guard **Hardwire** units as identified by TRC.

It may void the warranty if installed incorrectly. (See directional mounting illustration below.)

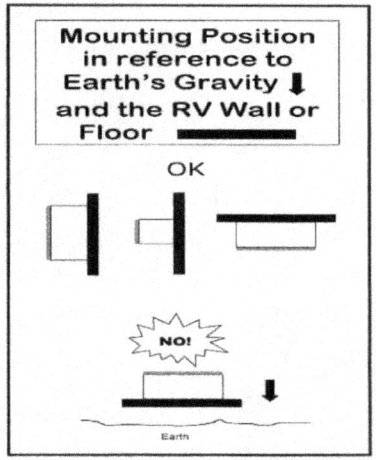

Apparently, TRC's "Standard" **Hardwire** Surge Guard Units should not be mounted with their backs (rear wall) oriented toward the ground (a.k.a. the cover facing upward). The WHY has never actually been divulged. However, I believe it's TRC's extra safety precautions concerning the contactors on the internal relay switch. If the back is "down," and if one of the springs that keep the contactors "open" should happen to fail, then gravity might, possibly, close the contactor and accidentally allow damaging, "bad" power into the RV.

By-Pass Key? Why the "By-Pass Key" feature is no longer installed on any of Southwire's/TRC's **Hardwire** models: A By-Pass Switch, engaged by an actual Key, was initially installed on the **Hardwire** units to allow the RV owner to be able to by-pass the unit when a Low Voltage situation was present (primarily to enable the charging of the battery/ies – NOTHING else turned on!). Once the By-Pass was activated, the unit only provided Surge Suppression. There was no protection for Hi/Low Voltage and Open Neutral in the By-Pass Mode. Unfortunately, because of an "out of sight – out of mind" propensity, most RV owners failed to take the unit out of By-Pass Mode after the need had passed. As a result, many an unprotected RV was "zapped" by a WIRING FAULT or Out-of-Spec Voltage. Consequently, as a protective measure, to assist the RVers, TRC phased out the By-Pass Switch and Key on subsequent production.

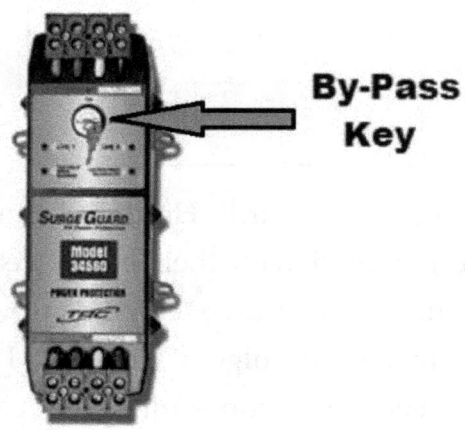

APPENDIX # 6

(November 9, 2015)

TRC's "Second Generation" of the "Standard"
Surge Guard RV Power Protection™

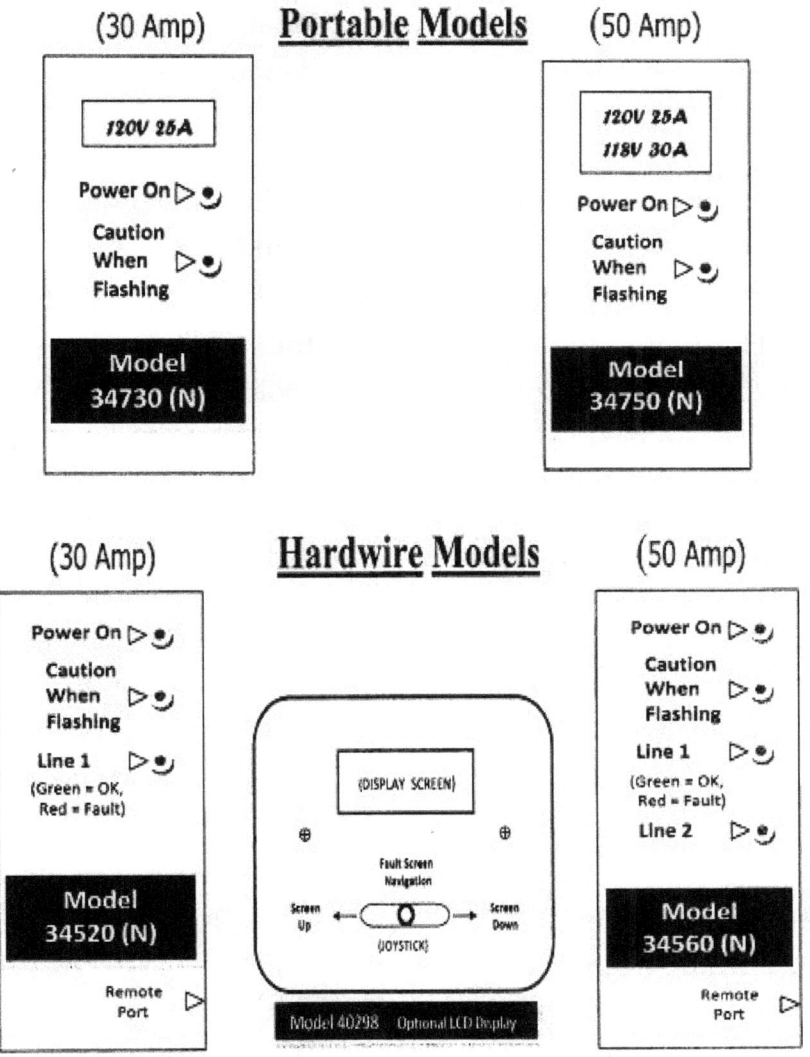

(N) – Is my particular designation for the "newer" version of the Model Number

The "Second Generation" of the "Standard" Surge Guard RV Power Protection units are illustrated on the previous page. The **Portable** units have "greenish" labels, and the **Hardwire** units have "orangish" labels.

The **Portable** 50 Amp and 30 Amp Models have a built-in two-line LCD display and two (2) lights (secondary backup for power and Fault indicators)

The **50 Amp Hardwire** Model has four (4) lights on the right side, which provide power and Fault indications to the user, while the **30 Amp Hardwire** has three (3) lights on the right side. Both Hardwire Models also have output jacks for an optional Remote Power Monitor LCD Display (Sold Separately – **Model: 40298**).

Features of TRC's "Second Generation" of the "Standard" **Surge Guard RV Power Protection**™

Both the **30 Amp and 50 Amp Portable** Models have two (2) LED lights on the right side of the front panel. From top to bottom, they are:

1. **"Power On" Light** – This input power indicator light will illuminate when power from the Post is supplied to the RV. Surge Guard's "safe" Voltage range is between 132 Volts maximum and 102 Volts minimum. If the Line Voltage is "out of spec" for more than 8 seconds, the Unit's Over/Under Voltage Protection monitor will prevent power from passing into the RV.

2. **"Caution When Flashing" Light** (Dual Purpose)

   a. **Time Delay Indicator** – This light blinks once per second for 2 minutes and 8 seconds (128 seconds) to indicate a prescribed time delay is "in progress" (this allows the Air Conditioner compressor to bleed off any head pressure).

   b. **Fault Indicator** – This light flashes if the unit has detected a "Miswired Post," "Reverse Polarity," or "Voltage on Ground Condition." (This WILL prevent power passing through a 50 Amp unit only.)

   (**Comment:** The Surge Guard literature states the unit will automatically shut "OFF" power for High/Low Voltage or an Open Neutral condition. However, when the "Caution" light is Fault Flashing [for situations other than Hi/Low Voltage or Open Neutral] the recommended solution is to find another power source! [i.e., Disconnect and then: **a**. move to a different site or **b**. start your generator.])

The **30 Amp Hardwire** Model has the same two lights listed above, plus one (1) additional light on the right side of the unit. **"Line 1"** – When *green*, the L-1 Voltage is between 132 Volts and 102 Volts. When *red,* the Voltage is above or below the specified range of Voltage, and power is shut "OFF" to protect your RV.

The **50 Amp Hardwire** Model has the same two lights listed previously, plus two (2) additional lights on the right side of the unit. **"Line 1"** & **"Line 2"** – Just like the 30 Amp Model, the Voltage is between 132 Volts and 102 Volts when green. When *red,* the Voltage is above or below the specified range of Voltage, and power is shut "OFF" to protect your RV.

Surge Suppression – All the 30 Amp and 50 Amp models have built-in Surge Suppression Modules. Their function is to protect against excessive transient Voltages (spikes). The 30 Amp Units are rated at 2,450 Joules, and the 50 Amp Units are rated at 3,850 Joules. This suppression capability protects the RV's 120-Volt electronic systems and appliances from harmful spikes without disrupting the RV's power supply.

The **Portable** models' built-in displays have the following readouts:

LCD Power Display Indicator – There are two alternating screens on the Surge Guard Display. The main screen and the secondary screen display different information.

1. **Main Screen, "Power Up"** – The top line will display "DELAY," and the bottom line will display the time delay's count-up, in increasing seconds, until it reaches 128.

2. **Main Screen, "Normal Operation"** – The 50 Amp Model will display Voltages and Amp Draws for L-1 and L-2. However, the 30 Amp Model only displays Voltage and Amp Draw for L-1; because there is no L-2.

   a. **Top Line of Text** – Displays information about L-1 in the following format: "xxx**V** yy**A**," where xxx and yy are numeric values, and "**V**" stands for Volts available, while "**A**" stands for Amps of current being drawn.

   b. **Bottom Line of Text** – Will display the Voltage and Amp Draw for L-2 (50 Amp only) in the same format as the top line of text.

3. **Secondary Screen, "Normal Operation"** – Shows RV STATUS ON or RV STATUS OFF on the top line and the Voltage of L-1 on the bottom line (e.g., L1 120V).

4. **Main Screen "Fault"** – If the Voltage coming into the RV is less than 102 on either L-1 or L-2, then the main screen will display: "L1 LOW" or "L2 LOW," instead of the Voltage and Amp Draw. If the Voltage coming into the RV is greater than 132, then the main screen will display: "L1 HIGH" or "L2 HIGH," instead of the Voltage and Amp Draw.

5. **Reverse Polarity** – If the Polarity of the Voltage coming into the RV is reversed, then the Surge Guard unit will display 'REVERSE' on the top line and 'POLARITY' on the bottom line until this condition is corrected. The "Reverse Polarity" screen will alternate with a "Faulty Ground" screen (same layout pattern).

The **Hardwire** models with the optional display installed *(Display Model # 40298 & Cable # 40258)* automatically exhibit the same Main Screens as the Portable models ("Power Up" and "Normal Operation"). However, during a "Fault" condition (e.g., when the Voltage on L-1 or L-2 is too high or too low), a separate set of L-1 and L-2 Voltage Screens, as well as the L-1 and L-2 Amp Draw Screens, can be displayed.

Pushing the joystick to the "Right" will scroll the "Fault" Screens (one screen at a time – push the joystick, again, to advance to the next screen) in the following order:

L-1 Voltage
L-2 Voltage
L-1 Amp Draw
L-2 Amp Draw
View Faults

Pushing the joystick to the "Left" will scroll the "Main" screens in reverse order.

When the "View Faults" screen is displayed, pushing "Down" on the joystick will cause recorded (stored) Faults in the unit's memory to display (one Fault at a time – push the joystick to the "Right" to advance to the subsequent Fault or "Left" to reverse the order). The most recent Fault to have been recorded is labeled as Fault 1, the Fault recorded prior to this is labeled as Fault 2, and so on. Thus, the unit can store up to 16 Faults before it discards the oldest Fault (Fault 16) in order to add a "new" encountered Fault (Fault 1). Pushing the joystick "Down" again will return the display to the "View Faults" screen.

Critical Note: An especially crucial mounting requirement for "Standard" Surge Guard **Hardwire** units as identified by TRC is illustrated on the next page:

It may void the warranty if installed incorrectly. (See directional mounting illustration below.)

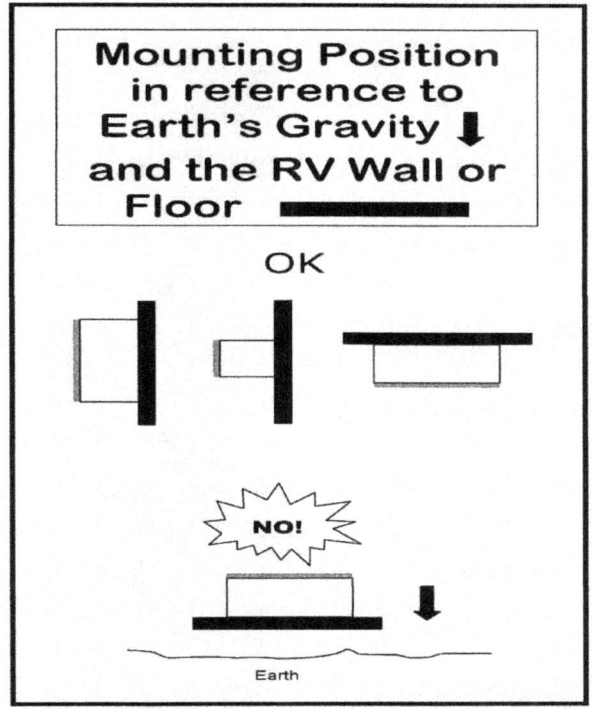

TRC's "Standard" **Hardwire** Surge Guard Units should not be mounted with their backs (rear wall) oriented toward the ground (a.k.a. the cover facing upward). The WHY has never actually been divulged. However, I believe it's TRC's extra safety precaution concerning the contactors on the internal relay switch. If the back is "down," and if one of the springs that keep the contactors "open" should happen to fail, then gravity might, possibly, close the contactor and accidentally allow damaging, "bad" power into the RV.

APPENDIX # 7

(August 3, 2018)

Southwire's "Third Generation"
of the "Standard Portable Models."
Surge Guard RV Power Protection™

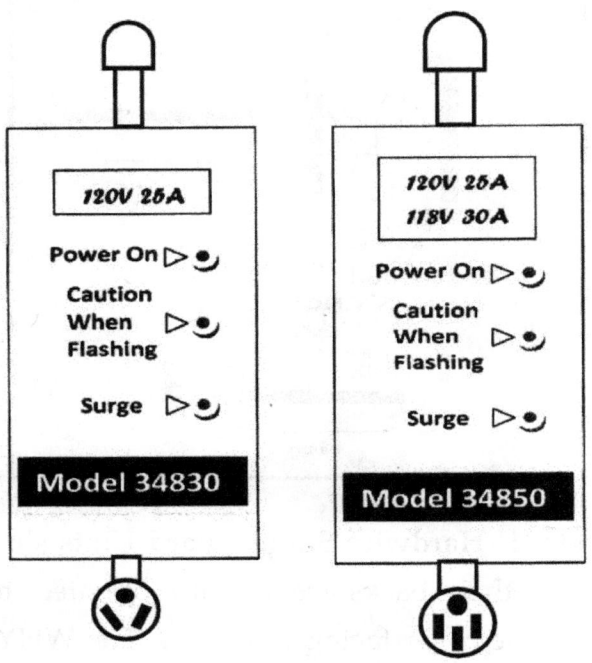

These **Portable** models have the same functionality as the **Portable** 34830(N) and 34850(N) models, except for the additional SURGE light. (See Appendix # 6)

Don't panic! I've been administering the Electricity Quiz on page viii for over two decades, at the beginning of my seminars at RV rallies, RV dealerships, and major RV parks. 99% of the participants have always circled most (if not all) of the incorrect answers.

The reason is simple. It's because using electricity in one's home is so commonplace; no one even thinks about it when they turn "ON" a switch. They simply "hit" the switch and always expect everything to "function" as it should. Therefore, every participant answered the questions according to their accustomed use of electricity in their home or workplace. Quite frankly, when it comes to electricity, that's everyone's primary frame of reference.

However, as I stated in the Introduction, using electricity in an RV is entirely different, as evidenced by the Correct answers to the questions. The test was meant to "shock" you toward understanding that dealing with electricity everywhere, with an automaton approach, is not enough. Hopefully, triggering you to start studying a different methodology – How to deal with electricity, "logically," as it pertains to RVs.

Please trust me. Once you learn as much as you can from this *Primer*, you will certainly appreciate just how differently electricity seems to work in an RV. Also, you'll enjoy your RVing experiences even more because the "electrical surprises" will be much easier to prevent or deal with.

(**Comment:** My wife and I don't consider the surprises as tragedies. They're just RV stories, and every RVer has, at least, one or two dozen of them!)

About Dale, the RV Tech, Teacher, & Author...

Dale Lee Sumner is a retired RVIA/RVDA Master Certified RV Service Technician and former owner/president of Mobile RV Medic, Inc.

He has sixty years of experience using and living in RVs (including more than a decade of recent "full-time" RVing) and conducting the business of repairing RVs. Now, he is concentrating on educating the RV owners.

And...Dale loves to teach what he writes! His goal is to provide as many RVers as possible – be they initially "Considering" RVing, just "Beginning" to RV, been "Camping" for years, or are living the dream of "Full-Timing" – with a solid, baseline understanding of the different (non-house-like) functional areas in their RVs.

Dale's teaching style is educational yet casual and entertaining. He writes in a down-to-earth, non-technical fashion so every reader can quickly become familiar with the subject(s).

I sincerely hope you enjoyed this book. If you did, please comment about it on social media and, surely, write an Amazon or Goodreads review.

And, of course, please tell a friend about this book — especially if your friend owns an RV or is thinking about getting one.

Thank you for your support,

Dale Lee Sumner

p.s. You may want to check out the **RV Blog** page on our website: sumdalus.com

www.ingramcontent.com/pod-product-compliance
Lightning Source LLC
Chambersburg PA
CBHW060802050426
42449CB00008B/1494